LOW-GLYCEMIC

Meals in *Minutes*

Fast Track Your Family to Healthy Eating and Active Living

Foreword by Ray D. Strand, M.D.

LAURA KALINA
Registered Dietitian

CHERYL CHRISTIAN
Certified Personal Trainer

Library and Archives Canada Cataloguing in Publication

Kalina, Laura, 1960-
    Low-glycemic meals in minutes : fast track your family to healthy
eating and active living / Laura Kalina, Cheryl Christian.

Includes index.
First published 2007 under title: Low-glycemic meals in minutes : reset
    your life with healthy eating and active living.
ISBN 978-1-895984-31-6

    1. Low-carbohydrate diet--Recipes. 2. Glycemic index.
I. Christian, Cheryl, 1961- II. Title.

RC662.K35 2008   641.5'6383   C2008-905271-4

True Health Global Publishing   Laura Kalina
1939 Tinniswood Court   231 Sunhill Court
Kamloops, British Columbia, Canada V2E 2K5   Kamloops, British Columbia, Canada V2E 2P5
www.LowGImeals.com   Tel: 250-372-0815
Tel: 250-374-0722

5th Printing

The recipes in this book have been carefully tested in our kitchen. For those people with food or
other allergies, or who have special food requirements or health issues, please read the suggested
contents of each recipe carefully and determine whether or not it may create a problem for you.
We cannot be held responsible for any hazards, loss or damage that may occur as a result of any
recipe use or menu plan. For those with special dietary needs, allergies, or health problems, in the
event of any doubt, please contact your medical advisor prior to using this book. No individual
should use the information in this book for self-diagnosis, treatment or justification in accepting or
declining any medical therapy for any health problem or disease.

Photography by Kelly Pape
Printing by Teldon Print Media

To purchase additional copies
of Low-Glycemic Meals in Minutes
or bulk orders
please visit our website:
www.LowGImeals.com

COVER Taco Salad in a Tortilla Bowl, Ricotta Cheesecake

Low-Glycemic Meals in Minutes
Fast-track Your Family to Healthy Eating and Active Living

Contents

Foreword

Today we are in the midst of the greatest health care crisis to hit the modern western world—obesity. What is even more concerning is the fact that it is now projected that over 30% of the next generation will develop diabetes sometime in their life. In this world of unparalleled medical information, many of us are dying and suffering needlessly because of lack of knowledge. How we choose to live our lives is a major factor in determining not only the length of our lives, but also our quality of life.

The most important aspect of our health is determined by the foods we choose to eat. It is becoming more and more obvious that the highly processed foods we are consuming today are one of the main reasons we are facing the obesity and diabetes epidemics. Learning to prepare and serve meals that contain good, low-glycemic carbohydrates along with good fats and proteins, is key to your health and the health of your family. When you combine a healthy diet with a modest exercise program and high quality nutritional supplements, you give yourself the absolute best chance of protecting your health and maintaining a healthy weight.

There are times when a book comes along that will greatly impact many lives. This book by Laura Kalina and Cheryl Christian is one of those books. The principles used to create the wonderful recipes found in this book are based on health concepts of low-G.I. eating. Dr. David Jenkins, a professor at the University of Toronto, fearlessly challenged the long-held concept of simple sugars versus complex carbohydrates as the way to determine how quickly our blood sugar rises following the intake of carbohydrates.

In 1981, Dr. David Jenkins released a study where he compared blood sugar levels following the ingestion of a particular carbohydrate to those following the ingestion of a control food (glucose). From the resulting differences in blood sugar levels emerged the concept of the "glycemic index." He gave glucose a glycemic index of 100 and all other foods tested were indexed based on how much they raised blood sugar. His findings shocked the medical community. He found that complex carbohydrates like bread, rice, cereals, and potatoes actually spiked our blood sugar much faster than table sugar.

Studies have revealed that 85 to 90 percent of the carbohydrates that adults and children are eating today in the U.S. and Canada are highly processed and high-glycemic. This has led us to repeatedly spike our blood sugar and eventually become much less sensitive to our own insulin. The insulin resistance that has developed because of our poor diet and lack of physical activity is the primary reason we are in the midst of not only an obesity epidemic, it is the major reason so many of us are becoming diabetic. It has now been shown that nearly 25 percent of the adult population has full-blown insulin resistance and another 25 percent are well on their way of developing it. This leads to a constellation of health problems that has been defined by the medical community as the "metabolic syndrome." These individuals develop high blood pressure, abnormal lipids, increased blood clotting, significant weight gain, and are at high risk of developing heart disease and diabetes. When this occurs, you not only begin aging much faster than you should, but you also gain an unusual amount of weight around your middle that you just can't lose. You begin to hold on to fat like a sponge holds on to water. This is all the result of an underlying resistance to your own insulin.

This cutting edge book provides you and your family with the guidance necessary to begin eating healthy low-glycemic carbohydrates like whole, fresh fruits and vegetables along with whole grains. The Phase 1 recipes allow you to not only break the damaging cycle of spiking blood sugar, but also allow you to have victory over your cravings and emotional eating. Over time, you actually become more and more sensitive to your own insulin again. When you combine healthy, low-glycemic carbohydrates with good fats and proteins, you allow your body the best opportunity to become more sensitive to your own insulin. This is especially true when you combine this healthy diet with a modest exercise program and high quality nutritional supplementation. Once you have successfully reached your weight and health goals, you are able to move on to Phase 2, which reintroduces healthy grains, potatoes, and cereals.

It is important to point out the fact that some of you are now gaining a fear of consuming carbohydrates because of the low- or no-carbohydrate diets that are permeating the book shelves. You must realize that our bodies need and desire good carbohydrates, which also contain all of those great vitamins, minerals, and antioxidants that our bodies need and require. Simply eating 8 to 12 servings daily of fruits and vegetables will decrease your risk of heart disease, stroke, diabetes, cancer, and Alzheimer's disease by two- to three-fold.

Laura and Cheryl make these recommendations so easy and obtainable. You now have a great resource of easy-to-prepare, healthy recipes that provide those good carbohydrates, good fats, and good protein. The food we consume is one of the greatest drugs we put into our body. Take the time to learn how to prepare these healthy, delicious recipes that will help reverse any carbohydrate cravings you may have and at the same time protect your health.

I think you will find that these innovative recipes not only taste great, they are also easy to prepare. Your family will enjoy the pleasure of sharing these meals together as everyone's health improves. Diets simply do not work. We need to learn how to prepare and eat healthy delicious food all over again. This book will make your task so much easier and so much more fun. The *Low-Glycemic Meals in Minutes* cookbook will be a valuable tool in your family's journey to optimal health.

Ray D. Strand, M.D.

www.healthyandleanforlife.com
www.drraystrand.com

Introduction

Congratulations, you have taken the next step towards a healthier you! Drawing from their extensive background, Cheryl Christian and Laura Kalina have come together to share their innovative, real-life-tested and family-approved formulas to ease you into a healthy lifestyle.

Cheryl Christian, as a Certified Personal Trainer, understands the need for families and individuals of all ages to make healthier choices when it comes to meal planning. As a busy mother of two boys, she also understands the overwhelming difficulties that many people face as they try to incorporate a healthy lifestyle into one that is already very demanding.

Through her desire to help her young, overweight son, Cheryl embarked on a lengthy personal journey of researching and experimenting to find a healthy weight loss plan. Low fat, low carbohydrate and in particular, calorie counting were among her first attempts to control his weight. Frustration followed as his weight continued to climb to unhealthy levels. Her search ended when she began studying the effects of weight management through low-glycemic eating. She discovered that his calorie consumption was not out of line, but an abundance of high glycemic carbohydrate choices was sabotaging their efforts. With this new found knowledge, Cheryl's next challenge was to adapt and incorporate dietary changes that could fit easily into their busy lifestyle. Her success in this is what motivated her to develop the "Pre-cook Days" and the "Quick Prep" meal plan that can easily be incorporated into any busy household. More importantly, Cheryl encouraged her children to participate in meal preparation. Using an "assembly-line" process, healthy pre-cooked proteins, and an array of low-glycemic carbs, including fresh fruits and vegetables, were lined up on the counter top. Good fats replaced the bad, and homemade snacks replaced rice cakes and instant noodle soups. Her children were taught how to assemble their own personal wraps, pitas and salads for healthy meals on the run. Their involvement allowed them to take ownership of their school lunches while keeping within some healthy boundaries. At the end of each day, Cheryl and her husband were able to put together a quick and delicious meal in minutes.

Another important factor in her son's transformation was the introduction of exercise, replacing some of the hours he normally spent playing video games. As his weight began to reduce, it was evident that the dietary changes and the Quick Prep method were working. It was with some amusement that Cheryl discovered the boys making extra wraps and selling them at school. Parents began to call and ask how the Quick Prep worked. She then realized the need for families and individuals to understand how low-glycemic eating can lead to lifelong weight management and better health. Perhaps even more importantly, her children now have the life skills to prepare healthy meals and include regular exercise as they live on their own as young adults. Whether you are a single person or have a large family to feed, you now have the opportunity to learn how to incorporate homemade healthy "fast food" into your daily meals.

Laura Kalina's passion for food, including the availability of healthy food for everyone, started in early childhood when she had aspirations of becoming a dietitian. Since achieving that dream, her contributions to food security and healthy eating have been many. Some of her career highlights include the creation of Shop Smart Tours Inc, the largest supermarket nutrition education program in Canada. Laura was instrumental in creating Community Gardens and Kitchens in her city, where families could come together to cook and share healthy meals for the week. Her book *Building Food Security in Canada* continues to be a sought after resource across North America.

As a registered dietitian and successful business leader, Laura has an extensive understanding of the role of food and nutrition in the prevention of chronic diseases, such as diabetes, heart disease and cancer. She has seen all too often the damaging effects of oxidative stress on the body

caused by hectic lifestyles, poor food choices, environmental pollution and a compromised food production system. As a busy mother herself, with two active teenagers, one of whom is a daughter with type 1 diabetes, she also understands the daunting challenges that families face trying to balance a multitude of activities with the goal of achieving optimal health.

The most common concern of today's busy families is "not enough time." Lack of time, combined with the convenience and prevalence of fast food restaurants and

Laura's children, Anya and Jake, enjoy getting involved in the kitchen – using the Quick Prep method, they can assemble a nutritious school lunch or snack in minutes.

prepackaged foods, has led to an unprecedented rise in obesity rates and chronic diseases such as type 2 diabetes and heart disease. Of particular concern is the tripling of childhood obesity in the last decade. This book will make your "not enough time" concern a thing of the past. It focuses on the "Quick Prep" method and shows you how easy it is to prepare healthy, well-balanced meals for your family in less time than a trip to your local fast food restaurant.

To help you achieve a healthy weight, *Low-Glycemic Meals in Minutes* also features nutrition tips throughout the book, a section on physical activity, cellular nutrition and a complete shopping list and sample menu plan. More than a cookbook, it will make the transition to well-being easy and fun for you and your family.

Benefits of Eating Together as a Family

Whether your family is large or small, traditional or non-traditional, or composed of unrelated roommates or friends, the benefits of eating together for mental and physical health are many. Even if you are single and often eat alone, take time to preprare and enjoy your food. You are worth it!

CATHY'S STORY

In our family, dinner is a time to connect and share what's happening in everyone's lives.

Cathy's family around the dinner table.

Meals together at home teach so many life skills to children. When they were young they learned about sorting and counting, putting dishes away in their proper places, how to set the table. They learned that when the last carrot is peeled we needed to write "carrots" on the grocery list. As children get older, they learn to be responsible for getting home on time for dinner, or calling to say if they won't be there. Our children have helped with meal preparation since they were in elementary school. While preparing meals we discuss the categories of food – meat, dairy, vegetables and fruit, grains – and their importance to our health. We have taught them how to prepare a meal on their own, to follow a recipe, and to plan ahead so that the various dishes are ready on time.

Meals are an excellent time to practice social skills such as recapping the events that day, telling about fun, embarrassing or interesting events, talking about travel, vacation and life plans. Discussions of current events that concern us all occur around the table at meal times. Communication is healthy for our self esteem – pair that with talking as a family everyday and *now* you are talking health!

BENEFITS OF EATING TOGETHER

Nutritional
- More fruit and vegetables
- Calicum-rich foods
- Fewer fried foods
- Less pop
- More low-G.I. foods
- Relaxed atmosphere which promotes better digestion
- Lowered risk of obesity
- Fewer eating disorders

Social
- Regular schedule encourages emotional well-being for children
- Sense of belonging and security
- Better performance and behaviour in school and workplace
- Better social skills
- Better vocabulary by age 5
- Less likelihood that children will grow up to smoke or use drugs and alcohol

Success Stories

KIM'S STORY

I have been battling my weight most of my life, always unhappy with the way I looked, and consequently missing out on things because of it (wouldn't go swimming with the kids, etc.). The many diet and exercise programs I tried didn't bring me a lot of success. Working out 3 to 4 times a week was making me stronger, but I still couldn't lose that extra 20 or 30 pounds. When I reached my 50s, I knew I needed to get serious. In June 2005, while at the gym, I overheard Cheryl Christian talking to a friend of mine. She was explaining her "Quick Prep method" which was shopping twice a week and going home and prepping the food right away. This ensured that when you opened your fridge, you had numerous low-glycemic healthy choices which took only 5 or 10 minutes to prepare.

One thing led to another, and Cheryl became part of my life. I signed her up as my personal trainer and began using her Quick Prep method, incorporating low-glycemic foods into my diet. I learned the importance of proper nutrition and how the Glycemic Index (G.I.) worked. The G.I. made so much sense to me. I broke my meals into 5 or 6 smaller portions and found I was never hungry. Quick Prep was very helpful, as I tend to have a busy schedule. I quickly found out that if I neglected my prep days, I would end up grabbing for something that wasn't a healthy choice.

This time the effort to lose the weight worked! The first 5 pounds didn't make much of an impact on me, because I have lost 5 pounds many times, but when I had lost 10 to 15 pounds, I was starting to feel great and needed to buy new clothes. I looked forward to my training sessions and weekly weigh-ins because of the results I was getting. It's not over yet, but to date I have lost close to 30 pounds. There is no question that it requires effort and hard work, but it's an incredible feeling when you see what you accomplish. It feels even better when you have everyone you know telling you how good you look. There is nothing quite like it!

A TEACHER'S STORY

As a high school District Resource Room teacher for students with autism and other related needs, I have attended conferences related to brain research including issues such as autism, ADD, and ADHD. Research has indicated that these individuals can increase their ability to focus with a higher protein, low-glycemic diet as well as using flaxseed oil daily to reduce aggression. As I began to research recipes that would

Debbie, District Resource Room teacher

be suitable, I met Cheryl Christian and purchased *Low-Glycemic Meals In Minutes*. Since then we have been using the low G.I. recipes in the classroom with some surprising discoveries. Overall, there has been a dramatic drop in behavioural issues. Staff has noticed students are easier to manage and are more willing to work towards a positive outcome. Over the months, students have become more able to control their impulses.

Initially, when parents inquired about the low-G.I. diet, it was explained that it is not a cure, but a lifestyle change. Our classroom goal was to develop a natural way to alter eating habits that directly affect how the brain functions, increasing individual capability to learn. We continue to witness individual growth in all areas.

HEALTHY EATING STARTS EARLY

As a young person, Leah remembers how difficult it was to get the whole family to eat together. "When I became a mom I wanted to be a role model for my family and encourage healthy eating

habits early!" Now with 3 small children, Leah and her husband see the benefits of preparing food in advance and having nutritious food available for the family.

"Breakfast has really changed in our family; I realize the importance of reducing those high-glycemic cereals and serving healthier choices. I want to set a good example for the kids and encourage eating that promotes a healthy weight," says Leah. Weight has been a struggle for her and she wants to ensure her family leads a healthier lifestyle.

The Jupp family at the dinner table.

TOM'S STORY

I am 48 years old and a captain in my city's fire department. Due to a biking accident, I was off work for 6 months, and the inactivity drove my weight up to around 240 pounds. Despite various attempts, I had a hard time losing the extra weight. Then I was introduced by my sister-in-law, a dietitian, to a five-day low-glycemic high-fiber cleanse, which included meal replacement shakes, nutritional bars and quality nutritional supplements.

Following the cleanse, I started on a 12-week trim down challenge (similar to the Phase 1 outlined in this book). This lifestyle change has been awesome for me. I wake up in the morning feeling energetic and continue to feel good throughout the day without insatiable carbohydrate cravings. I have the energy to exercise, spend time with my family, and socialize. I feel a renewed youthful exuberance and zest for life.

Tom lost 28 pounds in 12 weeks and now maintains a healthy weight.

Healthy Eating 101

All the recipes in this cookbook were developed to be low to moderate on the glycemic index (G.I.) with emphasis on healthy fats and proteins. The G.I. is simply a numerical system that rates how fast carbohydrates break down into glucose and enter the bloodstream. Low-G.I. foods are slowly digested and absorbed, which causes gentle rises in blood sugar and insulin levels. Lowering your insulin levels is not only a key factor in weight loss, but also the secret to long-term health. Low-G.I. foods, such as fruit, vegetables, legumes (beans and lentils) are also high in fibre, nutrients and antioxidants. Choosing low G.I. foods will help you to:

- control your appetite and cravings, as they tend to keep you feeling fuller, longer
- lose weight
- control your blood glucose levels and lower your risk of getting type 2 diabetes
- control your cholesterol levels and lower your risk of getting heart disease

STOP CARBOHYDRATE CRAVINGS

Carbohydrate cravings often lead to eating high-glycemic foods such as bread, rice, potatoes, commercial baked products and sweets (see table next page). As shown in the graph below, sugar from these foods is digested quickly and causes a rapid spike in blood sugar. This, in turn, triggers a surge of insulin which causes the blood sugar to drop into the hypoglycemic range. This leads to the release of stress hormones, which drives the blood sugar back up to normal but leaves an uncontrollable hunger, resulting in the need to to eat something. Usually it is another high-glycemic meal or snack, continuing the vicious cycle. If you start the day off with a high-glycemic meal, you may eat up to 80% more calories in the day. It is important to observe whether you are spiking your blood sugar with your food choices. Switching to low-glycemic eating will diminish carbohydrate cravings and help control your appetite which will ultimately help you lose weight.

Glycemic Index Tables

The Glycemic Index (G.I.) is a scale that ranks carbohydrate-rich foods by how much they raise blood glucose levels compared to a standard food. The standard food is glucose or white bread. A lot of starchy foods have a high glycemic index.

Choose low- and medium-G.I. foods more often.

Lower G.I. *Choose MOST*	Medium G.I. *Choose MORE often*	Higher G.I. *Choose LEAST*
BREADS		
Sprouted wheat bread or tortilla	Whole grain bread (coarse)	White bread and buns
Oat bran bread	Whole grain rye bread	Whole wheat flour bread
Heavy mixed grain bread	Whole wheat pita	Bagels
Pumpernickel	Whole wheat or flax tortillas	Croissants and baguettes
		Pancakes and waffles
CEREAL		
All Bran™	Grapenuts™	Bran flakes/corn flakes
Bran Buds with Psyllium™	Shredded Wheat™	Rice Krispies™
Slow cook oats	Quick oats	Cheerios™
Oat Bran™		Instant oats
Red River™		Commercial granola
Fibre 1™		
GRAINS		
Barley	Basmati rice	Short-grain and instant rice
Bulgur	Brown rice	Grits
Quinoa	Couscous	Canned pasta
	Parboiled or converted rice	Macaroni and cheese
	Pasta and noodles al dente	Instant noodles
OTHER		
Vegetables	Potato (red or new)	Potato, baking (Russet)
Fruit	Sweet corn	French fries
Black beans	Ryvita™ (rye crisps)	Pretzels
Lentils	Stoned Wheat Thins™	Rice cakes
Chickpeas	Black bean soup	Soda crackers
Kidney beans	Green pea soup	Granola bars
Split peas	Popcorn	Cake
Soy beans		Cookies
Skim milk		Fruit roll-ups
Soy milk		Candy and pop
Yogurt		Fruit juice
Whey protein powder		
Soya protein powder		
Nutrimeal™		

For more information on the glycemic index of other foods, go to www.glycemicindex.com

About the Book's Recipes

Low-Glycemic Meals in Minutes is divided into two sections: Quick Prep and 30 Minute Solutions. All of the kitchen tested recipes use the best carbohydrate, protein and fat choices to control hunger, aid in weight loss, maintain blood sugar levels, and improve overall health. The nutrient analysis is based on the average number of servings per recipe. If the recipe specifies 4 to 6 servings, the analysis is based on 5 servings.

Quick Prep recipes are family friendly and easy to prepare. With the emphasis on precooked proteins, chopped vegetables and a stocked pantry, healthy meals and snacks can be assembled with minimal effort. This book encourages children to feel comfortable in the kitchen and make healthy food choices. Recipes from the 30-Minute Solutions section require a little more time to prepare but still remain quick, convenient and uncomplicated.

PHASE 1 AND PHASE 2 GUIDELINES

During Phase 1 you need to avoid all sugars, breads, white flour, cereals, pasta, rice, and potatoes. You will have no restriction on natural fruits and vegetables. You will begin to appreciate what are considered to be good fats and good proteins. The initial phase of this program helps reduce carbohydrate cravings and reverses glycemic stress. Phase 1 helps regulate blood sugars and also has the great side effect of fat loss, putting one on the road to a healthy weight.

During Phase 2 you will be adding back into your diet foods that will not spike your blood sugar: whole grain breads and cereals, and certain rices, pasta and potatoes. (For examples refer to lower and medium GI foods listed on page 10.) These foods should always be consumed in moderation. You will continue to reverse your insulin resistance over time in the majority of cases. This phase can be considered a healthy *weight management* program.

A sample menu plan is provided on pages 106 and 107.

THE IMPORTANCE OF WHOLE/NATURAL FOODS

Cooking with natural foods offers tremendous nutritional value as well as excellent flavour. Natural food menus reflect both balance and a variety. Simply put, cooking with natural foods supports health and well-being. The following guiding principles have been used in the development of this book.

- Cook with ingredients as close as possible to their natural state with a minimum amount of processing (raw vs. cooked, fresh vs. canned, whole grains vs. refined flours).
- Avoid hydrogenated fats (trans fats) and processed foods.
- Choose locally grown fruits and vegetables when possible. (Support your local farmers!)
- Choose high-fibre foods.
- Utilize herbs and spices to complement the natural flavour of foods.

Quick Prep – Healthy Fast Food from Home

You arrive home after a busy day, ravenous, and without any plans for dinner. The family would love a nutritious home cooked meal, but no one has the time or energy. Have you ever wondered how restaurants can magically prepare many meals in a short time? Wouldn't it be great if you and your family could do the same?

Enter Quick Prep — the healthy meal solution. If you are willing to set aside a couple of hours per week for preparation, this book will show you how to stock your fridge and pantry with quick, ready to assemble meals for your family. This easy system will enable you to have healthy, nutritious meals everyday, in the same amount of time you would spend waiting for a restaurant order.

Better yet, get your family involved in cooking. Invite kids to read the recipes and help collect the necessary ingredients and utensils. Kids can help add ingredients, stir soups and set the table for the meal. Ask them to tell you what they think of the recipe — do they like the taste, color, texture and so on? With the Quick Prep method, kids will feel comfortable in the kitchen and learn how easy it is to assemble a healthy meal in minutes. Who could have imagined that placing your family on the road to well-being could be so easy?

THE QUICK PREP SOLUTION

Step 1 Plan two cook days per week, such as Sunday and Wednesday evenings.

Step 2 Cook two to four protein sources that you will use in Quick Prep recipes over the next three or four days. Amounts prepared will depend on family size. Store in airtight containers and place in fridge for quick meals. If you prefer using dried legumes over canned, prepare a batch and store in airtight containers.

Step 3 • Chop or slice fresh, cleaned vegetables. Place in airtight containers.

   • Prepare a large fresh salad. Try spinach and a variety of mixed greens. (Greens remain fresh and crisp if you add vegetables such as cucumbers, tomatoes, and zucchini just before serving). Store in airtight containers.

Step 4 Prepare salsas, spreads and healthy dressings for the up-coming week using fresh herbs.

You are now ready to assemble healthy meals for the week.

PREPARING PROTEINS

This section features common protein sources, such as, skinless chicken breasts, lean ground beef and poultry, canned fish and canned legumes. Broaden your family's menu planning with other healthy proteins such as, lean cuts of beef, lean pork (fat removed), wild game, quail, pheasant, wild salmon, and trout. Vegetarians know the value in other protein sources such as tofu, quinoa, legumes and grains. Look at the easy preparation methods laid out below and decide what proteins you wish to cook.

Poached Chicken Breasts

Skinless, frozen chicken breasts, as opposed to fresh, are often more economical for families. By poaching the chicken breasts, they remain juicy and tender for four days in the fridge.

1. *Place skinless, boneless chicken breasts in pot. Cover with water and bring to a boil. Reduce heat and simmer until cooked (approximately 30-40 minutes).*

2. *Rinse in sink until water runs clear.*

3. *Place cooked chicken breasts in storage containers and keep up to 4 days in the fridge.*

Extra Lean Ground Beef

Ground turkey or chicken can be substituted in many recipes. Experiment!

1. *Fry lean ground beef, chicken, turkey until fully cooked (approximately 20 minutes or until no longer pink).*

2. *Drain off excess fat. You may wish to rinse with hot water if beef has excess fat (optional).*

3. *Place cooked ground meat or poultry in storage containers for up to 4 days.*

Dried Beans, Peas and Lentils (Legumes)

1. *Dried Legumes are economical but require more preparation time.*

2. *Canned Legumes are quick and easy to use. Keep a variety on hand in your pantry.*

3. *Legumes are extremely versatile. Serve in salads, dips or main dishes. Bean Tortilla Pie, page 90, pictured.*

13

Fish

Fish is one of your best protein choices, particularly salmon, tuna, trout, mackerel and herring. These fish also provide an excellent source of omega-3 essential fatty acids. Fresh fish is wonderful but not always available, so canned fish is a great staple for your pantry. Cook fresh fish and keep remainder in storage containers for up to 4 days, or have canned fish available for Quick Prep meals.

PREPARING VEGETABLES

Keep an assortment of fresh vegetables, some prepped and ready to use in the Quick Prep recipes.

1. Wash an assortment of fresh vegetables.

2. Cut vegetables such as peppers, onions, and celery for quick use. You may choose to julienne, dice, or chop depending on the recipes you are planning to make.

3. Store in airtight containers.

Salsas and Spreads

Spice up wraps, soups and omelettes with homemade salsas, dressings, fresh herbs and spices.

Prepare salsas and spreads in advance. See pages 37 to 39.

Fresh herbs add flavour without the need to add extra salt, fats or sugars to recipes.

Tzatziki dip is delicious in pitas or wraps. See page 38.

NOTHING GOES TO WASTE

Before you begin the next prep day, use up remaining prepared foods in Clean Sweep soup, salad or stir-fry recipes. Be creative; create your own Clean Sweep recipe.

See recipes on pages 35 and 36.

FRIDGE & FREEZER PREP

Your fridge is now stocked with ready to use vegetables, low-fat proteins and condiments. Complete your fridge prep by having an assortment of fruit, low-fat dairy products, eggs, healthy oils (flaxseed oil), commercial condiments (low-fat mayonnaise, mustards, and low-fat dressings). A well organized fridge helps everyone find the necessary ingredients to make quick and tasty meals.

Your freezer should contain bags of frozen fruit and vegetables, good quality protein sources and ice for smoothies. Purchasing food storage containers in a variety of sizes is a must!

PANTRY

Your pantry should only be stocked with items that are low-glycemic, such as dried or canned legumes, slow cook oats, canned fish, salsas, tomato sauce and condiments. A shopping list has been provided on pages 114 and 115 for photocopying. It has been divided into two sections. You will find the fresh foods list has vegetables, fruit, soy and dairy products and proteins that you will need to restock on a weekly or bi-weekly basis. The pantry list focuses on staples, spices, and condiments for the fridge that will need replenishing less frequently. Avoid shopping without a list or when you are hungry. This will help you avoid the temptation to buy unhealthy snacks.

FOOD SAFETY

To keep food safe to eat and as tasty as possible, it must be stored and reheated properly. Refrigerate leftovers within two hours of preparation. Very hot items should be cooled at room temperature for about 30 minutes before being refrigerated. When reheating in a microwave, always transfer food to glassware first.

Storage Times for Prepared Foods

PRODUCT	REFRIGERATOR (40°F/4°C)	FREEZER (0°F/-17°C)
Cooked chicken pieces, plain	up to 4 days	up to 1 month
Cooked ground meat, meatloaf and meat casseroles	up to 4 days	up to 3 months
Soups and stews	up to 3 days	up to 6 months
Cooked poultry casseroles	up to 4 days	up to 4 months
Cooked fish	up to 4 days	up to 6 months
Combination dishes (such as lasagna)	up to 4 days	up to 6 months

Tips for Success

People often feel overwhelmed when they are told by their doctor that they need to make lifestyle changes to lower their risk of chronic disease – such as diabetes and heart disease. In Sheryl Giudici's clinical nutrition practice, this book has been a wonderful tool to help her clients achieve their health goals, particularly for weight loss. They learn to make easy, nutritious recipes that use real, whole foods. With a well stocked pantry and fridge, low-glycemic menu plan and shopping list, success comes easy.

Sheryl's clients report feeling satisfied, decreased cravings, better overall eating, and for many – weight loss. They feel that they are making permanent changes that will help them manage their weight into the future by creating healthier lifestyles for themselves and their families.

HERE ARE SOME TIPS FOR SUCCESS:

Eat a Low-glycemic Breakfast – Research shows that when you start your day off with a low-glycemic meal you eat fewer calories all day. Having a slow steady rise in blood sugars prevents mid-morning food cravings by ensuring that your blood sugar is kept within a healthy range. A great example of a low-GI breakfast is Bran Buds™, yogurt (with no sugar added) and fresh or frozen fruit mixed together.

Sheryl Giudici, Registered Dietitian, works in the area of weight management and the promotion of healthy eating.

Be Prepared – Don't be caught without healthy food choices at your finger tips. Always have a healthy snack with you, for example, an apple and a few almonds. Eat before you get really hungry – approximately three hours after your last meal or snack.

Power of Protein – It is important to have a protein choice at every meal and snack. Protein decreases the glycemic index of whatever carbohydrate you are eating, and also enhances the release of glucagon (your fat burning hormone). Another bonus is the fact that you will feel fuller, longer.

Watch Portion Sizes – It is important to understand what a serving size looks like.
- Two to three ounces of meat is the size of a deck of cards.
- 1 oz of cheese is the size of four dice
- ½ cup of cooked pasta is the size of a baseball cut in half
- a medium piece of fruit is the size of a tennis ball

Limit Alcohol – If weight loss is your goal, reduce or eliminate alcohol consumption as these empty calories can make weight loss very difficult.

Avoid Night Snacking – Having eaten low-glycemic foods throughout the day, your interest in night-time eating (i.e. carbohydrate cravings) should be reduced. Avoid eating two hours before bedtime as these calories are often stored as fat.

Quick Prep

Quick Prep Nutrition Shakes

Avoid the "I don't have time for breakfast" routine! Breakfast is truly one of the most important meals of the day. If you eat a low-glycemic breakfast you will have fewer carbohydrate cravings all day. With diminished carbohydrate cravings you can control your appetite, which will ultimately help you achieve a healthy weight. The following recipes take only minutes to make — so start your day off right!

LOW-GLYCEMIC SHAKE

Makes 1 serving

2 cups water
½ cup frozen berries
2 oz (60 g) strawberry or vanilla
   low-glycemic meal replacement powder
2 cups ice
1 tbsp ground flaxseed

In a blender, combine all ingredients and blend until smooth.

Calories 340 – CARBS 45g • PROTEIN 18g • FAT 9g • FIBER 9g

MOCHA LATTE SMOOTHIE

Makes 1 serving

1 cup cold coffee
1 cup low-fat milk
2 oz (60g) chocolate low-glycemic
   meal replacement powder
2 cups ice

In a blender, combine all ingredients and blend until smooth.

Calories 162 – CARBS 13g • PROTEIN 20g • FAT 3g • FIBER 4g

SHAKE ON THE RUN

Makes 1 serving

1 cup milk or water
1 container (175 g) sugar-free fruit yogurt
1 oz (30 g) vanilla or strawberry
   soy or whey protein powder
1 to 2 cups ice

Mix all ingredients in blender bottle and shake.

Calories 284 – CARBS 25g • PROTEIN 28g • FAT 8g • FIBER 1g

JAKE'S SHAKE

Makes 2 servings

1 cup low-fat milk
1 cup water
1 oz (30 g) vanilla soy powder
1 banana
1 cup unsweetened frozen mixed fruit
   (optional)
2 cups ice

In a blender combine all ingredients and blend until smooth.

Calories 185 – CARBS 27g • PROTEIN 17g • FAT 1g • FIBER 2g

PEANUT BUTTER CUP SMOOTHIE

Makes 1 serving

1 cup water
1 cup low-fat milk
2 oz (60g) chocolate low-glycemic
   meal replacement powder
1 tbsp natural peanut butter
2 cups ice

In a blender, combine all ingredients and blend until smooth.

Calories 300 – CARBS 31g • PROTEIN 19g • FAT 11g • FIBER 4g

Nutrition Tip

Looking for a low- glycemic meal replacement powder? Read labels and choose a company which tests the glycemic index of their products. Low- glycemic meal replacement powders should meet the following guidelines: protein should be the first ingredient listed and contain at least 12 – 15 grams of protein per serving; fat content between 5 – 7 grams per serving. Pay attention to the sugar source! Choosing one with fructose will have a lower glycemic index than glucose and maltose.

Sunrise High Protein Smoothie

Makes 1 serving

½ cup water
½ cup low-fat vanilla yogurt
½ cup fresh or unsweetened frozen fruit
   (strawberries, blueberries, raspberries,
   blackberries)
¼ cup orange juice
1 oz (30 g) vanilla soy or whey
   protein powder
1 tbsp ground flaxseed or flaxseed oil
2 cups ice

In a blender, combine all ingredients and
blend until smooth.

Calories 290 – CARBS 26g • PROTEIN 33g • FAT 6g • FIBER 5g

Tropical Cheesecake Smoothie

Makes 2 servings

1 can (10 oz/284 ml) mandarin orange
   segments with juice
1 can (14 oz/398 ml) pineapple in its own juice
1 cup low-fat cottage cheese or plain yogurt
½ cup orange juice
2 cups ice

In a blender, combine all ingredients
and blend until smooth.

Calories 310 – CARBS 50g • PROTEIN 17g • FAT 5g • FIBER 3g

Low-Glycemic Shake

Bananarama Tofu Boost

Makes 2 servings

1 ripe banana
½ cup dessert tofu (or fruit flavoured)
1 oz (30 g) vanilla soy or whey protein powder
1 cup low-fat milk
¼ tsp almond extract
2 cup ice

In a blender, combine all ingredients and
blend until smooth.

Calories 190 – CARBS 25g • PROTEIN 18g • FAT 1g • FIBER 1g

Lemon Tart Smoothie

Makes 2 servings

½ cup low-fat plain yogurt
1 tbsp lemon juice
½ cup unsweetened frozen strawberries,
   thawed
1 cup unsweetened grape juice or light
   cranberry/raspberry juice
2 oz (60 g) strawberry low-glycemic
   meal replacement powder
2 cups ice

In a blender, combine all ingredients and
blend until smooth.

Calories 235 – CARBS 41g • PROTEIN 11g • FAT 3g • FIBER 3g

Nutrition Tip

Soy protein is an excellent source of protein and contains
numerous phytonutrients with many health benefits. Look for
products that have 20 – 25 grams of pure soy protein isolate per
serving. Look for non-GMO i.e. soy that is not genetically modified.

Quick Breakfast Ideas

On-The-Run Breakfast

Phase 2 • Makes 1 serving

A Favourite

⅓ cup All-Bran™ or Bran Buds™
½ cup fresh fruit
½ cup cottage cheese (1% or fat-free)
    or low-fat yogurt (no sugar added)
2 tbsp sliced almonds

Mix in a bowl and enjoy.

Calories 340 – CARBS 43g • PROTEIN 24g • FAT 8g • FIBER 14g

Egg in a Nest (kid friendly)

Phase 2 • Makes 1 serving

1 slice whole grain bread
1 egg
2 tbsp cheddar cheese, grated
salt and pepper to taste

Coat frying pan with non-stick spray and heat over medium heat. Cut out center of bread in the shape of a circle (using a glass or a cookie cutter). Place bread into frying pan and break egg into center. Cover with lid, reduce heat to low, and cook until egg is done. Sprinkle cheese on top. Serve with salsa if desired.

Calories 225 – CARBS 20g • PROTEIN 13g • FAT 11g • FIBER 3g

Country Garden Omelette

Phase 1 • Makes 2 servings

✦ **Sauté in a 10-inch non-stick frying pan and cook until softened:**
1 tsp olive oil
½ cup assorted vegetables, finely chopped
    (onion, green or red bell pepper)

✦ **Beat together:**
3 eggs
2 tbsp skim milk
dash dried oregano and basil
salt and pepper to taste
2 tbsp sharp cheddar cheese, grated

Pour egg mixture over vegetables in pan and reduce heat to low. Cover and cook for a few minutes until eggs are fluffy and no longer runny. Top with grated cheese and cover for 1 minute.

Calories 115 – CARBS 5g • PROTEIN 11g • FAT 6g • FIBER 1g

For Phase 2, make a wrap by cutting omelette in pieces and placing in two 10-inch whole wheat or flaxseed tortillas. Top with salsa. Roll up and enjoy.

Country Garden Omelette

OLD FASHIONED OATMEAL

Phase 1 • Makes 2 servings

1 cup slow cook oats
1¾ cup water or skim milk
½ cup dried cranberries
2 tbsp sliced almonds, toasted

Bring water to boil, add oats and cranberries. Cover, turn off heat and let sit for 10 to 12 minutes without stirring. Add almonds just before serving.

Calories 285 – CARBS 40g • PROTEIN 16g • FAT 8g • FIBER 5g

HOMEMADE MUESLI

Phase 1 • Makes 2 servings

1 cup slow cook oats
¾ cup skim milk
¾ cup low-fat, sugar-free fruit yogurt
2 tbsp sliced almonds
¾ cup diced apple, pear or berries
sweetener to taste

In bowl, soak oats in milk. Place in refrigerator overnight. Add yogurt, almonds, fruit and sweetener to taste. Mix well.

Calories 320 – CARBS 43g • PROTEIN 15g • FAT 11g • FIBER 7g

FRENCH TOAST

Phase 2 • Makes 2 servings

1 egg
2 tbsp low-fat milk
½ tsp cinnamon
½ tsp pure vanilla extract
2 slices sprouted wheat bread

In a shallow dish, whisk egg, milk, cinnamon and vanilla. Dip 2 slices of bread into egg mixture. Cook in a non-stick frying pan on medium to high heat until lightly browned.

Calories 110 – CARBS 14g • PROTEIN 6g • FAT 3g • FIBER 1g

May serve with peanut butter and light jam, or yogurt and fruit.

Nutrition Tip

Eggs are high in protein and contain valuable nutrients such as vitamin A, magnesium, iron and riboflavin. Look for omega-3 enriched eggs. While more expensive than regular eggs, they are lower in saturated fat, higher in omega-3 fatty acids and contain more Vitamin E.

Spicy Pineapple Chicken

Quick Prep Meals

Quick Prep Poultry

These recipes use skinless, pre-cooked poultry that has been poached. Refer to cooking instructions on page 13. Many recipes are "kid friendly"— especially great for teens who arrive home hungry after school. These recipes are also great for entertaining unexpected company — a delicious meal ready in minutes.

SPICY PINEAPPLE CHICKEN

Phase 1 • Makes 4 servings

✦ ***Sauté 5 to 7 minutes in a large frying pan:***
1 tbsp olive oil
1 red bell pepper, cut in strips,
1 green bell pepper, cut in strips,

✦ ***Add:***
1 can (14 oz/398 ml) pineapple chunks with juice
1 cup salsa
2 tbsp cilantro or parsley, chopped
2 tsp grated fresh ginger or ¾ tsp ground ginger
2 cups cooked chicken, cubed

Continue to cook stirring frequently, until chicken is heated through. For a thicker sauce, mix 1 tsp cornstarch with 3 tbsp water and add to pan. Heat until thickened, stirring constantly. Add salt and pepper to taste.

Calories 215 – CARBS 18g • PROTEIN 23g • FAT 6g • FIBER 3g

Try serving over lightly cooked bean sprouts or chopped chinese greens for additional flavour.

QUICK CHICKEN SOUP

Phase 2 • Makes 4 to 6 servings

✦ ***Sauté in large pot until tender:***
1 tbsp olive oil
1 onion, chopped
2 stalks celery, chopped
2 carrots, chopped

Sprinkle 2 tbsp all-purpose flour over vegetables and stir for 2 minutes.

✦ ***Add and bring to a boil:***
4 cups or 1 carton (32 oz/900 ml) chicken broth
3 cups low-fat milk
¼ tsp each of dried sage, thyme and savory
1 tsp Worcestershire sauce
2 cups cooked chicken breast, diced

✦ ***Add:***
½ cup uncooked whole wheat pasta.

Reduce heat and simmer for 15 to 20 minutes.

Calories 272 – CARBS 21g • PROTEIN 28g • FAT 8g • FIBER 2g

Tips to Improve Your Kids' Nutrition

• Make a conscious effort to eat together as a family and keep meal times pleasant.
• Remember, parents are role models for healthy lifestyles.
• Monitor screen time (computer/TV). Not only are kids inactive in front of a screen, they are influenced by commercials for junk food. They will snack more while sitting in front of a screen than when they are playing.
• Have a general rule not to eat food anywhere in the house except in the kitchen or dining room.

Thai Chicken Tortilla Pizza

Phase 2 • Makes 4 to 6 servings

Preheat oven to 375°F.

✦ *Bake for 3 minutes on an ungreased cookie sheet:*

4 large whole wheat tortillas

✦ *Spread on each tortilla:*

1 to 2 tbsp Thai Peanut Sauce (page 38) or your favourite store-bought light peanut sauce

✦ *Sprinkle evenly over all 4 tortillas:*

2 cups cooked chicken, finely chopped

½ small red bell pepper, julienned

½ small green bell pepper, julienned

½ cup carrots, grated

1 cup low-fat mozzarella cheese, grated

Bake 10 to 12 minutes until cheese is completely melted and edges are lightly browned. If desired, broil for one minute to brown top. Use a pizza cutter to cut into wedges.

Calories 331 – CARBS 28g • PROTEIN 30g • FAT 11g • FIBER 3g

Asian Salad

Phase 1 • Makes 4 servings

✦ *Toss together in a large bowl:*

2 cups cooked chicken, cubed

3 cups shredded cabbage

1 cup mushrooms, sliced

2 carrots, grated

2 tbsp cilantro, chopped

1 cucumber, thinly sliced

½ cup non-fat oriental style salad dressing or Ginger-Sesame Dressing on page 56

black pepper to taste

✦ *Top with:*

3 green onions, thinly sliced

1 tangerine, divided into sections

Calories 225 – CARBS 16g • PROTEIN 25g • FAT 7g • FIBER 4g

Dijon Chicken

Phase 1 served over salad greens
Phase 2 served over rice or whole wheat pasta. Makes 4 servings

✦ *Sauté in a large frying pan, over medium heat:*

1 tomato, seeded and chopped

2 green onions, chopped

1 green bell pepper, sliced

¼ cup cilantro, chopped

⅓ cup dijon mustard

2 tbsp fresh lime juice

2 cups cooked chicken breasts, cubed

Serve over salad greens, rice or pasta.

Calories 144 – CARBS 5g • PROTEIN 23g • FAT 3g • FIBER 1g

You can substitute 1 cup of Big Batch Tomato Salsa (page 37) for the tomato, onion, pepper and cilantro.

Thai Chicken Tortilla Pizza

Indonesian Curried Salad

Phase 1 • Makes 4 servings

✦ **Stir together in a medium size bowl:**
2 cups cooked chicken, cubed
2 pears with skin, cubed
½ English cucumber with skin, chopped
2 green onions, chopped

CURRY DRESSING

✦ **Whisk together:**
¼ cup low-fat plain yogurt
¼ cup low-fat mayonnaise
1 tsp curry powder
½ tsp dry mustard
½ tsp ground allspice
½ tsp garlic powder
salt and pepper to taste

Stir chicken mixture and dressing together. Serve over salad greens.

Calories 213 – CARBS 14g • PROTEIN 23g • FAT 7g • FIBER 3g

Turkey Pesto Quesadillas

Phase 2 • Makes 6 to 8 servings

Preheat oven to 350°F.

✦ **Arrange in a single layer on baking sheet:**
4 large whole wheat tortillas

✦ **Top half a side of each tortilla evenly with:**
1 tbsp pesto (store-bought)
¼ cup parmesan cheese, grated
½ cup onion, chopped
1 large tomato, seeded and sliced
½ cup black olives, sliced
2 cups cooked turkey or chicken, chopped
1 pkg (10 oz/300 g) frozen chopped spinach, thawed with moisture squeezed out
½ cup feta cheese, crumbled
¾ cup low-fat mozzarella cheese, grated

Fold each tortilla over. Bake 15 to 20 minutes, or until tortillas are golden and cheese is melted. Cut each quesadilla into 6 wedges and serve with salsa and low-fat sour cream, if desired.

Calories 265 – CARBS 20g • PROTEIN 22g • FAT 11g • FIBER 3g

Quesadillas are good for lunches or snacks, and make a great party platter when cut into small wedges and arranged with small bowls of salsa and sour cream.

Indonesian Curried Salad

TURKEY CACCIATORE WITH PEPPERS

Phase 1 • Makes 4 servings

✦ **Sauté in a large non-stick frying pan for about 5 minutes until softened:**

1 tbsp olive oil
4 cloves garlic, minced
2 stalks celery, diced
1 large onion, chopped
1 red bell pepper, julienned
1 green bell pepper, julienned
½ tsp dried oregano
½ tsp dried thyme

✦ **Add:**

1 can (19 oz/540 ml) diced tomatoes

✦ **Whisk together:**

2 tbsp flour
1½ cup skim or 1% milk

Add to ingredients in frying pan, stirring constantly and heat until thickened (2 to 3 minutes).

✦ **Add:**

2 cups of cooked turkey, cubed
½ tsp each salt and pepper

Heat thoroughly. Serve with grated parmesan cheese.

Calories 270 – CARBS 24g • PROTEIN 28g • FAT 7g • FIBER 5g

FAST FUSION CHICKEN

Phase 1 • Makes 4 to 6 servings

✦ **Saute in a large, non-stick frying pan at medium-high heat until browned:**

1 to 2 tbsp olive oil
2 cups cooked chicken breast, cubed
½ large onion, chopped
2 cloves garlic, minced

✦ **Add and toss until thoroughly coated:**

1 tbsp curry powder

✦ **Add:**

1 red bell pepper, chopped
1¼ cups low-sodium chicken broth
⅓ cup raisins
2 tbsp tomato paste
1 tbsp lime juice

Reduce heat and simmer for 15 to 20 minutes or until thickened. Serve with side salad.

Calories 199 – CARBS 13g • PROTEIN 21g • FAT 7g • FIBER 3g

Phase 2 if served over basmati rice.

Nutrition Tip

Recipes like Turkey Cacciatore with Peppers provide two sources of protein: turkey and milk. Protein is an essential nutrient because it helps build and repair muscle, hair, nails and skin. Protein also lowers the glycemic index of a meal, which helps control blood sugar.

Quick Prep Ground Meats

Having cooked ground beef on hand makes it easy to come up with a quick meal solution. The recipes use extra lean ground beef that has been cooked and drained. You may substitute ground poultry or ground wild game. Always ensure that you have thoroughly cooked your ground beef, and then refrigerate.

MEDITERRANEAN PITA PIZZA

Phase 2 • Makes 6 to 8 servings

Preheat oven to 375°F.

✦ **Bake on a cookie sheet for 5 minutes until crisp:**
4 large whole wheat pitas

✦ **Mix:**
2 cups cooked ground beef, well crumbled
1 medium onion, minced
½ cup tomato sauce
1 tsp dried oregano
1 tsp dried basil
½ tsp each salt and pepper

✦ **Combine in separate bowl:**
1 large tomato, chopped
½ cup feta cheese (or mozzarella), crumbled
½ cup parmesan cheese, grated

✦ **Prepare garnish of:**
⅓ cup black olives, sliced

Layer a quarter of the meat filling onto each pita, then do the same with the tomato/cheese mixture. Sprinkle tops with sliced olives. Bake 12 to 15 minutes.

Calories 300 – CARBS 25g • PROTEIN 17g • FAT 15g • FIBER 4g

GROUND BEEF STROGANOFF

Phase 1 • Makes 4 servings

✦ **Sauté in a non-stick pan:**
1 tsp olive oil
1 onion, chopped
2 cloves garlic, chopped
1 green or red bell pepper, diced
2 cups fresh or 1 can (10 oz/284 ml) mushrooms, reserve juice

✦ **Add and simmer until heated through:**
2 cups lean ground beef, cooked
1 tbsp paprika
1 cup liquid (juice from canned mushrooms plus beef broth to make 1 cup)

✦ **Mix together:**
1 tbsp flour
4 tbsp low-fat sour cream or plain yogurt

Stir into stroganoff. Heat until sauce thickens.

Calories 344 – CARBS 11g • PROTEIN 30g • FAT 20g • FIBER 2g

Phase 2 if served with low-glycemic rice such as basmati, parboiled or brown, or over whole wheat pasta.

Mediterranean Pita Pizza

Jiffy Ground Beef Stir-fry

Phase 1 • Makes 4 servings

✦ **Sauté in a large non-stick frying pan over medium heat:**

1 tbsp olive oil

1 onion, chopped

3 cloves garlic, chopped

1 red bell pepper, julienned

2 cups broccoli, tops broken into florets and stems sliced

✦ **Add, then heat throughout:**

2 cups lean ground beef, cooked

1 tbsp fresh ginger, grated (or 1 tsp powdered ginger)

1 tbsp wine vinegar

¼ cup soy sauce

1 can (14 oz/398 ml) pineapple chunks, with juice

✦ **Blend in a small bowl:**

2 tsp cornstarch

¼ cup water

Add to beef mixture and stir until heated through.

Calories 280 – CARBS 27g • PROTEIN 22g • FAT 10g • FIBER 3g

Phase 2 if served over low-glycemic rice, such as basmati, parboiled or brown.

Quick Chili

Phase 1 • Makes 10 servings

✦ **Sauté in a stock pot:**

1 tbsp olive oil

1 onion, chopped

1 green bell pepper, chopped

3 cloves garlic, minced

✦ **Add:**

2 cups ground beef or chicken, cooked

1 can (19 oz/540 ml) kidney beans, drained and rinsed

1 can (19 oz/540 ml) romano beans, drained and rinsed

1 can (28 oz/796 ml) diced tomatoes with juice

1 can (5½ oz/156 ml) tomato paste

2 cups water

1 can (10 oz/284 ml) sliced mushrooms

1 to 2 tbsp chili powder (as desired)

1 tsp ground cumin

½ tsp salt

Bring to a boil, then simmer 20 minutes uncovered, stirring often.

Calories 260 – CARBS 30g • PROTEIN 25g • FAT 4g • FIBER 10g

Quick Chili

LETTUCE WRAPS

Phase 1 • Makes 6 servings

Wash one head of iceberg lettuce, dry and separate the leaves. Set aside.

✦ *Heat in a medium saucepan:*

2 cups cooked ground beef

2 green onions, chopped

1 red bell pepper, diced

1 can (7 oz/227 ml) water chestnuts, drained and chopped

✦ *Add:*

½ cup Thai Peanut Sauce (page 38) or your favourite store-bought light peanut sauce.

2 tbsp hoisin sauce

½ English cucumber, finely chopped

1 carrot, grated

Serve mixture in lettuce leaves by spooning a tablespoon into the middle. Lettuce wraps are designed to be eaten "taco-style."

Calories 236 – CARBS 15g • PROTEIN 17g • FAT12g • FIBER 3g

TACO SALAD IN A TORTILLA BOWL

Phase 2 • Makes 4 servings

Preheat oven to 375°F.

Form 4 small whole wheat tortillas into 4 fluted baking pans or 4 oven-proof 6-inch pyrex glass bowls. Bake 8 to 10 minutes or until lightly browned. Set aside.

✦ *Sauté for 5 to 7 minutes:*

1 tsp olive oil

1 small onion, chopped

1 clove garlic, minced

2 stalks celery, chopped

✦ *Add and heat throughout:*

2 cups cooked ground beef

1 cup salsa (store-bought or recipe page 37)

Layer tortilla bowl with meat mixture, store-bought refried beans or Black Bean Salsa (page 37) and shredded lettuce.

Garnish with low-fat sour cream, grated light cheddar cheese, and additional salsa if desired.

Calories 320 – CARBS 35g • PROTEIN 24g • FAT 12g • FIBER 5g

Taco Salad in a Tortilla Bowl

Tomato Spaghetti Sauce

Phase 1 served over spaghetti squash strands
Phase 2 served over cooked whole wheat pasta (½ cup per serving)
Makes 4 to 6 servings

✦ ***Sauté in a large pot:***
1 tbsp olive oil
1 medium onion, chopped
2 stalks celery, chopped
2 cups fresh mushrooms, chopped
   or 1 can (10 oz/284 ml) drained
2 cloves garlic, minced

✦ ***Add:***
1 can (5½ oz/156 ml) tomato paste
1 can (5½ oz/156 ml) water
1 can (28 oz/796 ml) diced tomatoes with juice
2 cups cooked ground meat
1 tsp dried basil leaves
2 tsp dried oregano leaves
1 tsp salt
½ tsp pepper

Simmer for 30 minutes or longer. Sprinkle with parmesan cheese when serving.

Calories 120 – CARBS 21g • PROTEIN 5g • FAT 3g • FIBER 6g

Hamburger Soup

Phase 1 • Makes 12 servings, 1 cup each

✦ ***In a large stock pot on medium heat, mix:***
2 cups cooked ground beef
1 can (28 oz/798 ml) diced tomatoes
1 can (19 oz/540 ml) kidney beans
1 can (10 oz/284 ml)) tomato sauce
1 can (10 oz/284 ml) mushrooms
5 cups water
1 medium onion, chopped
2 carrots, chopped
2 celery stalks, chopped
1 tsp Worcestershire sauce
½ tsp hot pepper sauce
½ tsp freshly ground pepper

Bring to boil. Reduce heat and simmer covered for about 35 minutes.

✦ ***Add:***
2 small zucchini, chopped

Simmer 10 minutes longer. Serve.

Calories 246 – CARBS 31g • PROTEIN 17g • FAT 6g • FIBER 12g

For Phase 2 add ½ cup whole wheat pasta or barley. If using barley, add with vegetables. If using pasta, add with zucchini.

Tomato Spaghetti Sauce

Quick Prep Canned or Cooked Fish

We do not always have the luxury of fresh fish, so the following recipes feature canned fish. Leftover fresh fish can be substituted in any of the recipes, just match quantities of the fresh fish to tin sizes. When tasty food is easy to make, older kids and teens will get into the action. Quick Prep makes the healthy choice the easy choice, and will curtail the endless trips to the cupboard at snack time for chips, cookies and crackers.

TUNA SALAD MIX

Phase 1 with lettuce or salad
Phase 2 in wrap or pita
Makes 3 to 4 servings

✦ **Mix:**
2 tins (6 oz/184 g each) water packed tuna, drained
¼ cup low-fat mayonnaise
2 dill pickles, chopped
2 green onions, minced
1 celery stalk, chopped

Serve over a bed of lettuce greens, in wraps or in pitas.

Calories 159 – CARBS 6g • PROTEIN 22g • FAT 5g • FIBER 2g

Teens can make this as a nutritious after school snack. It is easy to make, low-glycemic and low-fat.

CURRIED TUNA PIZZA

Phase 2 • Makes 4 servings

✦ **Mix:**
⅓ cup low-fat mayonnaise
1 tsp lemon juice
½ tsp curry powder

✦ **Add:**
1 tin (6 oz/184 g) water packed tuna, drained
1 stalk celery, finely chopped

✦ **Spread mixture over:**
4 whole wheat tortillas, 6-inch

✦ **Sprinkle evenly with:**
1 cup low-fat mozzarella cheese, grated
2 green onions, chopped

Broil 4 to 5 minutes or until lightly browned.

Calories 330 – CARBS 30g • PROTEIN 23g • FAT 13g • FIBER 3g

TUNA BURGER

Phase 1 served with salad
Phase 2 in whole grain bun or pita
Makes 4 servings

✦ **Mix:**
2 tins (6 oz/184 g each) water packed tuna, drained
1 egg
1 cup whole wheat bread crumbs
1 small onion, chopped
2 cloves garlic, minced
1 tbsp soy sauce
1 tbsp light teriyaki sauce
1 tbsp ketchup

Shape into patties. Sprinkle ½ cup cornmeal on a dish and coat patties on each side. Fry patties in 1 tbsp olive oil for about 6 minutes per side or until browned and heated through. Serve with a fresh lemon wedge and Light Tartar Sauce (page 39), or in a whole wheat bun or pita.

Calories 241 – CARBS 25g • PROTEIN 28g • FAT 4g • FIBER 3g

Nutrition Tip

The health benefits of fish have been widely established; it is a relatively inexpensive source of high-quality protein, low in saturated fat and contains omega-3 fatty acids, touted for their heart-protective benefits. Predatory fish such as shark, swordfish, fresh and frozen tuna, albacore tuna (not canned light tuna), have higher levels of mercury and should be consumed only occasionally. Canned light tuna contains species of tuna such as skipjack, yellow fin, and tongol, which are relatively low in mercury. Canned light tuna also tends to be lower in price which is an added bonus.

Italian Tuna Sauce

Phase 1 served over spaghetti squash strands
Phase 2 served over cooked whole wheat pasta
Makes 4 servings

✦ ***Bring to boil:***
1 can (19 oz/540 ml) stewed tomatoes
1 zucchini, chopped
1 tsp garlic, crushed
1 tsp Italian seasoning

✦ ***Add:***
2 tins (6 oz/184 g each) water packed tuna,
  drained

Boil gently, uncovered, stirring often until
thickened.

Calories 145 – CARBS 11g • PROTEIN 24g • FAT 1g • FIBER 2g

Toss with 2 cups spaghetti squash strands (Phase
1) or 2 cups cooked whole wheat pasta (Phase 2).
Sprinkle with fresh or grated parmesan cheese.

Nutrition Tip

Salmon is an excellent source of omega-3 fat. Research has
shown that omega-3 fat in fish helps protect us against heart
disease and cancer, and that fish oil can enhance the immune
system and suppress cancer cell growth. The best way to get
omega-3s is by eating cold water fish such as salmon, trout and
sardines. To boost your omega-3s, take a pharmaceutical grade
fish oil supplement.

Salmon Salad Fajitas

Phase 1 served over shredded lettuce
Phase 2 in whole wheat tortillas or pitas
Makes 4 servings

✦ ***Combine in a mixing bowl:***
1 tin (7½ oz/231 g) salmon, drained
2 tbsp low-fat mayonnaise
¼ cup low-fat plain yogurt
¼ tsp chili powder

✦ ***Add, stirring gently:***
1 carrot, grated
1 green onion, chopped
1 tomato, diced
½ cucumber, diced
¼ cup cilantro leaves, chopped
salt and pepper to taste

Calories 130 – CARBS 6g • PROTEIN 13g • FAT 6g • FIBER 1g

Salmon Waldorf Salad

Phase 1 • Makes 4 servings

✦ ***Combine in a bowl:***
2 tins (7½ oz/231 g each) salmon, drained
2 celery stalks, diced
1 large apple, chopped
½ cup walnuts, broken

DRESSING
✦ ***Stir together in a separate bowl:***
½ cup low-fat mayonnaise
¼ cup low-fat plain yogurt
1 tsp lemon juice
½ tsp dried thyme
¼ tsp each salt and pepper

Stir dressing into salad and serve.

Calories 294 – CARBS 12g • PROTEIN 17g • FAT 21g • FIBER 3g

SALMON LOAF

Phase 2 · Makes 4 to 6 servings

Preheat oven to 350°F.

✦ *Mix:*

2 cups leftover cooked fish or 2 tins
   (7½ oz/231 g each) salmon, drained

½ cup whole wheat bread crumbs

2 eggs, beaten

1 cup milk

1 tsp dill weed

1 cup onion, finely chopped

1 cup celery, finely chopped

5 shakes of Tabasco sauce

1 tsp salt (if not using canned fish)

Place mixture into a loaf pan or muffin tins
sprayed with cooking spray. Bake 40 minutes
for a loaf or 25 minutes in muffin tins.

Calories 246 – CARBS 14g · PROTEIN 25g · FAT 10g · FIBER 2g

TUNA CITRUS SPINACH SALAD

Phase 1 · Makes 4 servings

✦ *In a large bowl combine:*

1 can (10 oz/284 ml) mandarin oranges,
   drained

5 cups baby spinach leaves, washed and torn
   into pieces

½ Spanish onion, thinly sliced in rings

2 tins (6 oz/184 g each) solid water packed
   tuna, drained

DRESSING

✦ *Mix in a glass jar:*

1 tbsp sugar

½ tsp salt

1 tbsp dijon mustard

2 tsp lemon rind, grated

¼ cup fresh lemon juice (juice of 1 lemon)

2 tbsp flaxseed oil

Pour dressing over salad, toss to coat. Sprinkle
with ⅓ cup toasted almonds.

Calories 230 – CARBS 16g · PROTEIN 24g · FAT 8g · FIBER 2g

Tuna Citrus Spinach Salad

33

Mix and Match Wraps and Pitas

Mix and Match is a wonderful way to teach children how to prepare healthy lunches and snacks. By adding ingredients in an assembly line fashion, kids can choose their favourite fillings and toppings. Mix and Match recipes are Phase 2. For a Phase 1 recipe, use a lettuce leaf to wrap.

Choose a whole grain, flax, or sprouted wheat tortilla or pita pocket. Preheat in a microwave for 5 to 10 seconds before filling to make it easier to roll.

STEP 1

Place 2 to 3 oz (approximately ⅓ cup) protein of your choice onto the bottom third of each wrap or inside a pita.

STEP 2

Add your favourite chopped vegetables or fruit.

STEP 3

Dress it up with salsas, spreads or sauces (see pages 37 to 39).

STEP 4

Sprinkle with your favorite extras.

STEP 5

Wrap by folding in two sides, then folding bottom up over filling and roll until tight.

| STEP 1 | STEP 2 | STEP 3 | STEP 4 |
PROTEIN	**VEGGIES/FRUIT**	**DRESSING**	**EXTRAS**
Ground beef	Tomato Lettuce	Tzatziki Sauce (page 38) Hummus	Feta cheese
Chicken	Bean sprouts Onion Carrots	Black Bean Salsa (page 37) Tomato Salsa (page 37)	Low-fat cheese
Turkey	Bell peppers	Thai Peanut Sauce (page 38)	Hot sauce
Fish canned or fresh (tuna, salmon)	Avocado	Low-fat sour cream Natural peanut butter Sesame seed butter	Olives
Eggs	Celery	Low-fat mayonnaise	Pickles
Tofu	Zucchini Mushrooms	Low-fat commercial dressings	Spices
Legumes	Pineapple		
Cottage cheese	Strawberries Apples Pears Bananas	Low-fat plain yogurt	

Quick Prep "Clean Sweep" Leftovers

After 3 to 4 days, you are likely to have some odds and ends left in the fridge. There is no need to discard them if the vegetables and proteins have remained fresh. The following recipes are just a few ways to use up the remaining Quick Prep foods in a stir-fry, soup or salad. Experiment and create your own unique recipe!

CLEAN SWEEP STIR-FRY

Phase 1 • Makes 4 to 6 servings

✦ ***Whisk in a glass bowl then set aside:***
1 tbsp soy sauce
⅓ cup orange juice
2 tbsp hoisin sauce
½ tsp cornstarch

✦ ***Slice:***
5 to 6 cups assorted vegetables (red and green bell peppers, carrots, celery, zucchini, cauliflower, broccoli, mushrooms, bean sprouts, snow peas, peas, green beans, shredded cabbage or water chestnuts)

✦ ***Sauté in a large frying pan or wok over medium-high heat:***
1 tbsp olive oil
2 small onions, cut into wedges
1 clove garlic, minced
1 tbsp fresh ginger, chopped

Add firmer vegetables first, stirring constantly. Add remaining softer vegetables and cook 2 to 3 minutes or until firm vegetables are tender crisp. Pour soy mixture into vegetables. Cook 1 to 2 minutes or until thickened. Sprinkle with toasted almonds or sesame seeds.

Calories 98 – CARBS 16g • PROTEIN 3g • FAT 3g • FIBER 4g

Option: Add any available protein (chicken, beef) to make a complete meal.

CLEAN SWEEP SOUP

Phase 1 • Makes 10 servings

✦ ***Sauté in a stock pot until soft:***
1 tbsp olive oil
1 medium onion, chopped
3 cloves garlic, chopped

✦ ***Add:***
10 cups chicken, beef or vegetable stock
5 cups assorted vegetables, chopped (green bell peppers, diced tomatoes, cabbage, carrots, celery, green beans, etc.)
¼ cup parsley, chopped
1 tsp each salt and pepper
1 tsp dried thyme
1 tsp oregano
1 bay leaf
Worcestershire, hot sauce or salsa to taste

Bring to a boil, reduce heat. Cover and simmer for 45 minutes to 1 hour or until vegetables are tender.

Calories 50 – CARBS 8g • PROTEIN 1g • FAT 1g • FIBER 2g

Options:
• *Add left over protein, such as turkey, chicken, beef, or tofu to this soup for a complete meal.*
• *Add 1 can (19 oz/540 ml) beans, dried split peas or lentils to increase protein content.*
• *For a Phase 2 recipe, add ½ cup rice, ½ cup whole wheat pasta or ⅓ cup barley.*

Clean Sweep Salad

CLEAN SWEEP SALAD

Phase 1 • Makes 4 to 6 servings

Clean Sweep Stir-fry

✦ **Mix in a bowl:**

3 cups salad greens

1 red onion, sliced

3 cups vegetables, chopped (red, green or yellow bell peppers, broccoli, cauliflower, grated carrot, celery, tomato, cucumber)

½ cup feta cheese, crumbled

DRESSING

✦ **Mix:**

¼ cup fresh lemon juice (juice of 1 lemon)

2 tbsp olive oil

1 clove garlic, minced

2 tbsp dried oregano, crumbled

Pour dressing over vegetables.

Calories 129 – CARBS 10g • PROTEIN 4g • FAT 9g • FIBER 3g

Add leftover protein such as chicken, turkey, beef or eggs for a complete meal.

CLEAN SWEEP COLESLAW

Phase 1 • Makes 10 servings

✦ **Toss together in a large bowl:**

7 to 8 cups green or purple cabbage, shredded

1 cup carrots, grated

ORANGE VINAIGRETTE DRESSING

✦ **Mix in a small bowl:**

2 cloves garlic, crushed

1 tbsp dried parsley

¼ cup white vinegar

½ cup orange juice

¼ cup flax oil

2 tsp sugar or sweetener of choice

½ tsp salt

freshly ground pepper to taste

NUT TOPPING (OPTIONAL)

✦ **Combine in a small bowl:**

¼ cup sunflower seeds

¼ cup pumpkin seeds

¼ cup dried soya nuts

½ cup sliced almonds

Pour 2 to 3 tbsp of dressing over 1 to 2 cups of coleslaw mixture. Top with 2 tbsp nut topping.

Calories 186 – CARBS 10g • PROTEIN 5g • FAT 14g • FIBER 3g

Store-bought bags of coleslaw mix make this salad extremely quick to prepare. There will be enough dressing for additional salads throughout the week.

Clean Sweep Soup

Quick Prep Salsas, Spreads and Dips

A great way to enhance the flavour of many dishes is to keep fresh salsas and spreads at your fingertips. If you take the time to prepare some of the low-G.I. recipes in this section, you will have a variety of mix-and-match sauces for the up-coming week. Spice up wraps, pitas and meals with a burst of flavour!

Big Batch Tomato Salsa

Phase 1 • Makes 30 servings

✦ ***In a large non-metal bowl combine:***

6 large tomatoes, seeded and diced

2 red bell peppers, minced

2 green bell peppers, minced

1 sweet white onion, minced

1 tsp jalapeno pepper, minced

½ cup white vinegar

1 can (5.5 oz/156 ml) tomato paste (use only if you want thicker salsa)

4 garlic cloves, minced

½ cup fresh cilantro, chopped (optional)

3 tbsp lime juice (fresh squeezed is best)

2 tbsp lemon juice (fresh squeezed if possible)

1 tsp chili powder

1½ tsp dried oregano

1 tbsp dried parsley

1 tsp salt

1 tsp pepper

Cover and refrigerate for at least 1 hour, or overnight for flavours to blend. Keeps up to 4 days refrigerated.

Calories 17 – CARBS 4g • PROTEIN 1g • FAT 0g • FIBER 1g

This salsa can be used as a dip, or in pitas, wraps, omelettes, chili and taco bowls, and in "clean sweep" recipes. Be creative!

Black Bean Salsa

Phase 1 • Makes 20 servings

✦ ***Combine in a medium bowl:***

1 can (19 oz/540 ml) black beans, rinsed and drained

1 can (12 oz/341 ml) corn kernels, drained

2 tomatoes, diced

1 small onion, finely chopped

1 tbsp olive oil

2 tbsp cider vinegar or lime juice

3 tbsp cilantro or parsley, finely chopped

2 clove garlic, minced

¾ tsp cumin powder

½ tsp salt

black pepper to taste

Gently toss together.

Calories 102 – CARBS 19g • PROTEIN 5g • FAT 1g • FIBER 4g

Fruit Salsa

Phase 1 • Makes 10 servings

✦ ***Combine in a bowl:***

½ large grapefruit, sectioned and diced

2 tbsp red onion, finely chopped

⅛ tsp hot pepper flakes

1 tsp honey

1 tbsp lemon juice

1 cup fresh or thawed blueberries

2 tbsp cilantro, chopped

Mix gently, then serve immediately.

Calories 30 – CARBS 8g • PROTEIN 0g • FAT 0g • FIBER 1g

Fruit salsa is great over fish or chicken.

Big Batch Tomato Salsa

THAI PEANUT SAUCE

Phase 1

✦ *In a saucepan, combine:*
¼ cup natural peanut butter
¼ cup light soy sauce
2 tbsp lemon juice
2 tsp sesame seed oil
2 tsp fresh ginger, grated
1 tbsp honey
1 tsp garlic powder
pinch of hot pepper flakes

Heat over medium heat until bubbling, stirring constantly. Remove from heat and let cool. Store in fridge.

1 tbsp = Calories 39 – CARBS 2g • PROTEIN 1g • FAT 3g • FIBER 0g

For a quick dinner, pour Thai Peanut Sauce over cooked chicken and place under broiler for 5 to 7 minutes. Serve with vegetables.

FAST VEGGIE DIP

Phase 1

✦ *Combine in a bowl:*
2 cups low-fat sour cream
½ package onion soup mix
¼ cup low-fat mayonnaise

1 tbsp = Calories 17– CARBS 1g • PROTEIN 1g • FAT 1g • FIBER 0g

Makes a great dip for vegetables and pita chips, and as a spread in pitas and wraps.

Nutrition Tip
Garlic contains powerful immune supporting, cancer-fighting and heart health properties. When used in cooking, more that 70 sulphur-bearing compounds are released. The compounds hinder cancer cell growth and have antiviral, antibacterial and antifungal properties.

FAT FREE BLACK BEAN DIP

Phase 1

✦ *Place in a blender and puree until smooth:*
1-19 oz/540 ml can black beans
½ cup salsa

✦ *Spoon dip into a bowl. Stir in:*
¼ cup plain fat free yogurt
1 tsp fresh lemon juice
¼ tsp cumin
2 tbsp chopped fresh cilantro

1 tbsp = Calories 16 – CARBS 3g • PROTEIN 1g • FAT 0g • FIBER 3g

Works well with fat free sour cream, too. Serve with baked chips or cut veggies.

DIP WITH A TWIST

Phase 1

✦ *Combine in a bowl:*
1 cup low-fat plain yogurt
1 tsp dried dill
¼ tsp garlic powder

1 tbsp = Calories 8– CARBS 1g • PROTEIN 1g • FAT 0g • FIBER 0g

Makes a vegetable dip that combines a sweet flavour with a garlic "twist."

FRUIT DIP

Phase 1

✦ *Combine in a bowl:*
1 cup low-fat vanilla yogurt
1 tsp cinnamon
¼ tsp nutmeg

1 tbsp = Calories 12– CARBS 2g • PROTEIN 1g • FAT 0g • FIBER 0g

Makes a unique dip for assorted fresh fruits!

TZATZIKI SAUCE

Phase 1

✦ **Combine in a bowl:**

1¼ cup low-fat plain yogurt
¼ cup low-fat mayonnaise
juice of 1 lemon (¼ cup)
3 cloves garlic, minced
½ tsp salt

✦ **Add:**

1 cucumber, peeled, seeded and diced then
   patted dry with a paper towel
salt and pepper to taste

1 tbsp = Calories 8 – CARBS 1g • PROTEIN 1g • FAT 0g • FIBER 0g

HUMMUS

Phase 1

✦ **With a food processor or hand mixer, combine:**

1 can (19 oz/540 ml) chickpeas, drained
2 green onions, chopped
3 cloves garlic, chopped
¼ cup fresh lemon juice
   (juice of one lemon)
¼ cup peanut butter or tahini
   (sesame seed paste)
½ cup low-fat plain yogurt
½ tsp ground cumin
½ tsp salt
pepper to taste

Blend well. Serve chilled or at room
temperature with raw vegetables and
pita bread. Garnish with chopped
onions, tomato, or parsley.

1 tbsp = Calories 45 – CARBS 6g • PROTEIN 3g • FAT 1g • FIBER 1g

LIGHT TARTAR SAUCE

Phase 1

✦ **Stir together in a small bowl:**

½ cup plain yogurt
⅓ cup low-fat mayonnaise
3 tbsp dill pickle, chopped
1 tsp lemon juice
½ tsp dijon mustard
dash hot pepper sauce
dash Worcestershire sauce

Cover and refrigerate. Serve with fish or on
fish burgers.

1 tbsp = Calories 24– CARBS 1g • PROTEIN 1g • FAT 2g • FIBER 0g

*This sauce can be stored in a well-sealed
container or jar up to 5 days.*

Hummus

39

Flaxseed Pancakes

30 Minute Solutions

30 Minute Solutions

The following recipes require a little more time to prepare, but are well worth the effort. Each section is packed with a variety of nutritious, low-glycemic meals. There is something to please the palate of every member of the family. Categories include brunch ideas, soups, salads and dressings, as well as main meals, meatless meals and side dishes. And last but not least, there are always the finishing touches of a few desserts and snack ideas.

Flaxseed Pancakes

Phase 2 • Makes 4 servings   *Calories 220 – CARBS 37g • PROTEIN 10g • FAT 4g • FIBER 9g*

1¼ cup	whole wheat flour
½ cup	ground flaxseed
1 tbsp	cinnamon
1 tbsp	sugar
1 tbsp	baking powder
1¾ cup	skim milk
1	egg
1 tsp	vanilla extract

1. In a large bowl, mix whole wheat flour, ground flaxseed, cinnamon, sugar, and baking powder. Set aside.

2. In a medium bowl, whisk together skim milk, egg and vanilla. Pour wet mixture into flour mixture and stir until combined.

3. Heat a large non-stick frying pan over medium-high heat. Spray with oil before spooning batter into pan. Reduce heat to medium-low. When tiny bubbles appear on top side of pancake, flip and cook for approximately 2 more minutes or until golden and cooked through.

4. Serve with toppings such as fresh fruit, no-sugar jams, or 1 tsp peanut butter or almond butter.

In order to release the oil in flaxseed, it is necessary to grind the seeds into flax meal. All it takes is a few seconds in a coffee grinder.

Nutrition Tip

Flaxseed is one of the best sources of omega-3 fat, fibre and lignans. Lignans are plant compounds with hormone-like activity (also referred to as phytoestrogens). They are especially important in the fight against hormone-sensitive cancers like breast and prostate cancer. Regular consumption of flaxseed has been associated with reduction of total cholesterol and LDL (bad) cholesterol levels. Aim to add ground flaxseed to your diet on a regular basis.

Hearty Oatmeal Pancakes

Phase 2 • Makes 4 to 6 servings   *Calories 227 – CARBS 32g • PROTEIN 9g • FAT 6g • FIBER 4g*

½ cup	slow cook oats
½ cup	low-fat plain yogurt
½ cup	skim milk
2	large eggs
1 tbsp	canola oil
2 tbsp	brown sugar, packed
½ tsp	salt
1 tsp	baking powder
1 cup	whole wheat flour

1. In a medium bowl, combine oats, yogurt and milk. Set aside for 15 to 20 minutes to let the oats soften.

2. When the oats are finished soaking, beat in the egg and oil; mix well. Add the sugar and salt, then baking powder and flour. Stir until just moistened. For best results, let the batter stand for 5 minutes before cooking.

3. Heat a lightly oiled or non-stick griddle over medium heat (375°F for an electric frying pan).

4. For each pancake, pour about ¼ cup batter onto the griddle. Turn when the tops are covered with bubbles and look dry.

5. Serve with applesauce or yogurt.

Egg and Tofu Scramble

Phase 1 • Makes 2 to 3 servings   *Calories 169 – CARBS 8g • PROTEIN 14g • FAT 9g • FIBER 2g*

2	eggs
1 pkg (350 g)	extra firm tofu, crumbled
½	medium white onion, finely chopped
½	red bell pepper, diced
1 cup	mushrooms, chopped
¼ tsp	turmeric
½ tsp	salt

1. Beat eggs with tofu, set aside.

2. Sauté onion, pepper and mushrooms in a large non-stick frying pan over medium heat.

3. Add egg/tofu mixture, turmeric and salt. Stir until cooked.

4. Serve with salsa.

About Tofu

Tofu, made from the milk of soybeans, is a versatile, convenient food that can be made into a meal in minutes. It can be scrambled, stir-fried, baked, or added to soups, stews, shakes, lasagna and burritos. Tofu can be purchased in extra firm, firm, medium firm, medium soft or silken textures. Read the labels and purchase a variety with added calcium. Many food products are made from tofu, including soy cheese and meat substitutes.

COOKING TOFU
- Drain excess water from tofu before using it. For medium firm tofu, let it sit in a colander for 10 minutes or pat dry with a paper towel before using.
- Always cook tofu over low heat and do not over-cook it. Over-cooking causes tofu to become dry and tough.
- Marinate tofu in a glass or enamel dish; a metal dish may leave an unpleasant taste.

STORING TOFU
After tofu is opened, store the unused portion in the fridge immersed in water, where it will stay fresh for three to four days. Tofu is perishable and must be kept refrigerated.

BENEFITS OF SOYBEANS
The soybean has a unique composition offering a good balance of nutrients including high quality protein, fiber and essential fatty acids such as omega-3. Soybeans are often referred to as the best protein source originating from the soil. Soy is the only legume that contains a complete protein that is almost equivalent in quality to the protein found in dairy and meat products. Soy also contains isoflavones that may provide protection against heart disease, certain forms of cancer and osteoporosis.

Bean Burritos

Phase 2 • Makes 4 servings   *Calories 290 – CARBS 48g • PROTEIN 11g • FAT 6g • FIBER 7g*

1 tbsp	olive oil
½ cup	onion, finely chopped
1 clove	garlic, finely chopped
½ tsp	ground cumin
½ tsp	chili powder
1 can (19 oz/540 ml)	kidney beans, drained and mashed
1 tbsp	vinegar
to taste	salt (if desired)
4	whole wheat or sprouted grain tortillas (8-inch)

1. Heat oil in non-stick frying pan. Add onion and garlic and sauté until softened.

2. While stirring over medium heat, add cumin, chili powder, mashed beans and vinegar. Cook until heated through.

3. Divide bean mixture evenly among 4 tortillas.

4. Top with the following items:
   • a small amount of low-fat grated cheddar cheese
   • salsa
   • low-fat sour cream
   • tomatoes
   • shredded lettuce

5. Roll up and serve.

Bean Burrito

Egg Tortilla Bowls

Phase 2 • Makes 6 servings   *Calories 248 – CARBS 29g • PROTEIN 14g • FAT 9g • FIBER 2g*

8	eggs
2	green onions, chopped
½ cup	red bell pepper, chopped
⅓ cup	skim milk
to taste	salt and pepper
6	whole wheat tortillas (small, 6 to 8 inches)
⅓ cup	low-fat cheddar cheese, grated

1. Preheat oven to 375°F.

2. In a medium size bowl, whisk together eggs, green onions, red pepper, skim milk, salt and pepper.

3. Place tortillas into deep muffin tins or small oven-safe bowls (one per bowl). Pour egg mixture into tortillas. Sprinkle with cheddar cheese.

4. Bake 30 minutes or until centre is set. Let sit for approximately 5 minutes before serving.

Option: Add ½ cup salsa to eggs rather than green onions and red bell pepper.

Bake in fluted baking pans to dress up this dish.

Nutrition Tip

Flax, whole wheat or sprouted wheat tortillas make a lower glycemic alternative to traditional breads.

Egg Tortilla Bowl

Amazing Quiche

Phase 2 • Makes 4 to 6 servings   *Calories 168 – CARBS 14g • PROTEIN 14g • FAT 6g • FIBER 2g*

4	large eggs
1½ cups	1% milk
¼ cup	whole wheat flour
3 tbsp	cornmeal
3	green onions, chopped
½	red bell pepper, finely chopped
1 cup	low-fat cheddar cheese, grated
½ tsp	salt
½ tsp	black pepper

1. Preheat oven to 400°F. Spray a 9-inch pie plate with vegetable oil.

2. In a blender or food processor, combine eggs, milk, flour and cornmeal. Blend for 30 seconds, until well blended.

3. In the prepared pie plate, gently toss green onions, red pepper, grated cheese, salt and pepper. Pour the milk and egg mixture over the cheese mixture.

4. Bake 30 minutes, or until a knife inserted in the center comes out clean.

Nutrition Tip

Adequate intake of both calcium and vitamin D can reduce the risk of developing osteoporosis. Both children and adults need 1000 to 1500 mg of calcium daily, depending on age. In terms of food, that means consuming at least 3 servings of milk products every day. One serving includes 1 cup milk or enriched soy milk, ¾ cup yogurt, or 1½ oz cheese. Most people can't get enough calcium and vitamin D in their diets, so we recommend a pharmaceutical grade calcium supplement containing magnesium and vitamin D.

Homemade Turkey Sausage Patties

Phase 1 • Makes 8 to 10 patties   *Calories 108 – CARBS 4g • PROTEIN 12g • FAT 5g • FIBER 1g*

½ cup	slow cook oats
¼ cup	minced onion
1½ tbsp	dried parsley
1½ tsp	salt
1 tsp	black pepper, freshly ground
1 tsp	dried sage
½ tsp	ground cloves
½ tsp	ground nutmeg
2	eggs
1 pound	lean ground turkey

1. In a small bowl, combine oats, onion, parsley, salt, pepper, sage, cloves and nutmeg.

2. In a medium bowl, beat egg with a fork. Add turkey and oats mixture; mix well. Shape into 4 to 6 patties about ½ inch thick.

3. Preheat frying pan over medium heat. Place patties in preheated pan and cook for 5 minutes. Flip and continue cooking for 5 to 7 minutes, or until no longer pink inside.

Homemade Turkey Sausage Patties

Nutrition Tip

Ground turkey and chicken are lower-fat alternatives to ground beef. For food safety, ensure that the ground meat is cooked throughout and is no longer pink, or until food thermometer registers 165°F or 71°C .

Minestrone Soup

Phase 2 • Makes 8 servings   *Calories 160 – CARBS 30g • PROTEIN 5g • FAT 2g • FIBER 6g*

1 tbsp	olive oil
1	large onion, chopped
3	medium carrots, sliced
2 stalks	celery, sliced
3 cloves	garlic, finely chopped
1 cup	cabbage, chopped
1	red potato, peeled and diced
1 can (19 oz/540 ml)	kidney or romano beans
1 can (28 oz/796 ml)	tomatoes
6 cups	water or beef broth
1 tsp	dried oregano
1 tsp	dried basil
½ cup	whole wheat macaroni, uncooked
to taste	salt and pepper
	parmesan cheese, grated

1. In a large pot, sauté onion, carrots, celery and garlic in the oil until tender.

2. Drain and rinse the beans.

3. Add the cabbage, potato, beans, tomatoes, water, oregano and basil.

4. Bring to a boil; then reduce the heat. Cover and simmer for 30 minutes or until vegetables are tender.

5. Add the pasta. Cook over low heat for 15 minutes or until the pasta is tender.

6. Add salt, pepper or other seasonings if needed. Sprinkle with parmesan cheese before serving.

• *Rutabaga or zucchini can also be added to this soup.*

• *For added protein, add ½ pound of ground beef and sauté with the vegetables.*

• *To make beef, poultry or vegetable broth use commercial bouillon cubes, paste, or the low-sodium canned version. When using canned broth, dilute with ½ water to lower the sodium.*

Minestrone Soup

Black Bean Soup

Phase 1 • Makes 8 servings   *Calories 160 – CARBS 24g • PROTEIN 7g • FAT 4g • FIBER 5g*

2 tbsp	vegetable oil
2 stalks	celery, chopped
1	large onion, chopped
3	medium carrots, chopped
3 cloves	garlic, finely chopped
1 tbsp	ground cumin
1 can (28 oz/796 ml)	diced tomatoes
6 cups	water
2 cans (19 oz/540 ml)	black beans, rinsed and drained
1 tsp	salt
¼ tsp	hot pepper flakes (or to taste)

1. In a large pot, sauté celery, onion, carrots and garlic in the oil until softened. Stir in cumin and sauté 1 minute longer.

2. Stir in the tomatoes, water and black beans. Bring to a boil, then reduce heat. Cover and simmer for 30 minutes.

3. Add salt and hot pepper flakes to taste.

4. Serve topped with a spoonful of plain yogurt or fresh salsa (optional).

This soup keeps up to 4 days in the fridge or 4 months in the freezer.

• *Any 19 oz/540 ml can of beans can be used in place of black beans.*

• *To give a smoother texture, ladle out a portion of the soup and mash with a potato masher or purée in a blender or food processor, then stir back into the soup.*

Black Bean Soup

Soups

Red Lentil Soup

Phase 1 • Makes 6 servings   *Calories 180 — CARBS 25g • PROTEIN 9g • FAT 0g • FIBER 5g*

1 cup	dried red lentils, rinsed and drained
2	onions, coarsely chopped
5 to 6 cups	water or vegetable stock
1	bay leaf
2 cloves	garlic, minced
1 tsp	dried thyme (or 1 tbsp fresh chopped)
3	carrots, sliced thinly
3 tbsp	fresh parsley, chopped
1 tsp	salt
to taste	pepper

1. In a large saucepan, combine lentils, onions, water, bay leaf and garlic. Cover and bring to a boil. Reduce heat and simmer for 20 minutes.

2. Add thyme and carrots. Simmer covered for 30 additional minutes or until carrots are tender and lentils are soft.

3. Remove bay leaf. Add parsley, salt and pepper to taste.

Nutrition Tip

Lentils are a great source of fibre, B vitamins and protein, without excessive calories. They can be cooked quickly and, unlike dried beans, do not need to be soaked. Lentils come in red, brown and green. Brown and green hold their shape better and are usually used in salads and loaves. On the other hand, red lentils, which break down during cooking, are used in sauces and soups. The combination of lentils with a grain provides a complete protein.

Red Lentil Soup

Split Pea Soup

Phase 1 • Makes 8 servings   *Calories 218 – CARBS 36g • PROTEIN 14g • FAT 2g • FIBER 15g*

1 tbsp	olive oil
1	onion, chopped
3	carrots, chopped
3 stalks	celery, chopped
2 cloves	garlic, minced
2 cups	green or yellow split peas or a mixture of both
½ tsp	dried thyme
4 cups	vegetable or chicken broth
3 cups	water
1 tsp	salt
1 tsp	black pepper

1. In a large pot, heat the oil over medium heat. Sauté onion, carrots, celery and garlic in the oil until softened.

2. Add the split peas, thyme, broth and water. Bring to a boil, then reduce heat. Cover and simmer for 1 to 1½ hours until the peas are tender.

3. Add salt, pepper and other seasonings as needed.

For Phase 2, add ½ cup barley and add more water if desired.

Pea soup is wonderful when flavoured with a ham bone. Make the broth ahead of time by simmering the ham bone in water, then cool and skim fat.

Soups

Nutrition Tip

Legumes (such as chickpeas, beans and lentils) are an excellent source of soluble dietary fiber which helps in the regulation of blood sugar and in lowering blood cholesterol levels. Other sources of soluble fiber include oat bran, oatmeal, brown rice, barley, and pectin rich fruits (apples, strawberries and citrus fruit).

Curried Sweet Potato and Cauliflower Soup

Phase 1 • Makes 4 to 6 servings　　　*Calories 154 – CARBS 31g • PROTEIN 3g • FAT 2g • FIBER 3g*

3 cups	sweet potato, chopped
2 cups	cauliflower, chopped
2 tsp	garlic, crushed
2 tsp	olive oil
1 cup	onion, chopped
1 tsp	curry powder
½ tsp	cinnamon
⅛ tsp	salt
4 cups	vegetable stock

1. Place sweet potato and cauliflower in a microwave-safe dish with ½ cup water. Cover and microwave for 8 to 10 minutes, or until vegetables are tender. Set aside.

2. Sauté garlic and onion in oil in a large stock pot over medium-high heat until softened.

3. Add curry, cinnamon, salt.

4. Combine onion and sweet potato/cauliflower mixture in a food processor and purée until creamy smooth.

5. Pour all ingredients back into the stock pot. Add vegetable stock and heat to desired temperature, adding additional stock if desired.

6. Garnish with cilantro and low-fat sour cream.

Orange Carrot Soup

Phase 1 • Makes 4 servings   *Calories 150 – CARBS 21g • PROTEIN 3g • FAT 6g • FIBER 4g*

2 tbsp	non-hydrogenated margarine
½ cup	onion, chopped
4 cups	carrots, sliced
4 cups	vegetable stock
½ cup	orange juice
½ tsp	nutmeg
¼ tsp	black pepper
1 cup	skim milk
¼ cup	low-fat sour cream (optional)

1. In a large stock pot, sauté onions in margarine over medium heat for 5 to 6 minutes until softened.

2. Add carrots and stock; bring to a boil. Reduce heat and simmer for 15 to 20 minutes. Stir in orange juice, nutmeg and pepper.

3. Transfer soup to a food processor or blender and purée until smooth.

4. Return soup to stock pot; stir in milk. Simmer over low heat for 2 to 3 minutes until heated through.

5. Stir in 1 tbsp sour cream per serving (optional).

Orange Carrot Soup

Creamy Roasted Vegetable Soup

Phase 1 • Makes 6 servings   *Calories 100 – CARBS 12g • PROTEIN 1g • FAT 5g • FIBER 2g*

2 cups	squash, roasted *
1 cup	vegetables, roasted *
½ cup	water
4 cups	vegetable or beef broth
1 tsp	ground cumin
1 tsp	dried basil
1 tsp	dried oregano
1 tsp	salt

1. In a food processor, blend squash, roasted vegetables and water.

2. Pour contents into a large stock pot.

3. Add vegetable broth and spices. Bring to boil and simmer for 10 to 15 minutes.

* For roasting instructions see page 81.

Glycemic Index vs. Glycemic Load

The glycemic index (GI) is a numerical system to measure the rise in circulating blood sugar a carbohydrate triggers—the higher the number, the greater the blood sugar response. So, a low GI food will cause a small rise, while a high GI food will trigger a dramatic spike.

The glycemic load (GL) is a relatively new way to assess the impact of carbohydrate consumption that takes the glycemic index into account, but gives a fuller picture than does glycemic index alone. A GI value tells you only how rapidly a particular carbohydrate turns into sugar. It doesn't tell you how much of that carbohydrate is in a serving of a particular food. The carbohydrate in watermelon, for example, has a high GI. But there isn't a lot of it, so watermelon's glycemic load is relatively low. A GL of 20 or more is high, a GL of 11 to 19 inclusive is medium, and a GL of 10 or less is low. Foods that have a low GL almost always have a low GI. Foods with an intermediate or high GL range from very low to very high GI.

Basic Salad and Dressings

Phase 1 • Makes 2 servings   *Calories 45 – CARBS 10g • PROTEIN 2g • FAT 0g • FIBER 3g*

1½ cups	salad greens (romaine, leaf, boston, spinach)
1	small carrot, grated
½ cup	red, yellow or green bell pepper, diced
1	plum tomato, cut into wedges
½ cup	cucumber, sliced
¼ cup	red onion, chopped

Toss above ingredients in a small bowl. Serve with 2 tablespoons of one of the following dressings or use your favourite low-fat dressing.

LOW-FAT DRESSINGS

ORANGE VINAIGRETTE

Makes 1 cup

2 cloves	garlic, crushed
¼ cup	fresh parsley, chopped (or 1 tbsp dry)
¼ cup	white vinegar
½ cup	orange juice
¼ cup	flax oil
2 tsp	sugar
½ tsp	salt

freshly ground pepper to taste

In a small jar or blender, add garlic, parsley, vinegar, orange juice, flax oil, sugar, salt and pepper to taste. Mix well.

2 tbsp = Calories 70 – CARBS 3g • PROTEIN 0g • FAT 6g • FIBER 0g

YOGURT DILL DRESSING

Makes 2 cups

1½ cups	low-fat plain yogurt
¼ cup	low-fat mayonnaise
1 tbsp	white vinegar
1 tsp	dried dill weed (or 3 tbsp fresh)
⅓ cup	fresh parsley, chopped
1 tsp	dijon mustard
1 clove	garlic, minced

fresh ground pepper

In a small jar or bowl, combine all ingredients and whisk well. Covered and refrigerated, this dressing will keep up to a week.

2 tbsp = Calories 24 – CARBS 2g • PROTEIN 1g • FAT 1g • FIBER 0g

Salads

Basic Salad with Cranberry Vinaigrette

CRANBERRY VINAIGRETTE

Makes 1 ½ cups

½ cup	dried cranberries
2 cloves	garlic, crushed
1 tbsp	olive oil
½ tsp	salt and pepper
½ cup	orange juice
¼ cup	balsamic vinegar
¼ cup	flaxseed oil (or olive oil)

In a frying pan, place cranberries, garlic, oil, salt and pepper and cook over medium heat. Stir constantly. When ingredients come to a boil, reduce heat and cook for 2 minutes. Transfer to a bowl. Add orange juice, balsamic vinegar and oil. Let cool while preparing salad. Pour over salad and toss well.

2 tbsp = Calories 54 – CARBS 2g • PROTEIN 0g • FAT 5g • FIBER 0g

GINGER-SESAME DRESSING

Makes 1 cup

¼ cup	rice vinegar (or white vinegar)
¼ cup	orange juice
2 tbsp	low-sodium soy sauce
2 tbsp	peanut butter
1 tbsp	sesame oil
1 tbsp	brown sugar
1 tsp	garlic, crushed
2 tsp	fresh ginger, grated (or 1 tsp ground)

Combine all ingredients in a blender and purée until smooth. Chill 2 hours before serving.

2 tbsp = Calories 48 – CARBS 4g • PROTEIN 1g • FAT 4g • FIBER 0g

All of these dressings are low-fat because the oil has been partially replaced by orange juice, low-fat yogurt or low-fat mayonnaise.

Yogurt Dill Dressing, Cranberry Vinaigrette, and Orange Vinaigrette

Basic Coleslaw

Phase 1 • Makes 4 to 6 servings   *Calories 59 – CARBS 8g • PROTEIN 1g • FAT 3g • FIBER 2g*

4 cups	cabbage, shredded (about half a medium cabbage)
2	medium carrots, grated
½ cup	onion, finely chopped

DRESSING

1 tbsp	flaxseed oil
3 tbsp	white vinegar
1 tsp	salt
1 tsp	sugar

1. In a medium bowl, combine cabbage, carrots and onion.

2. Dressing: In a small bowl or jar, mix together oil, vinegar, salt and sugar. Pour over salad.

Try the Orange Vinaigrette dressing on page 55 as a zesty alternative.

Salads

Basic Coleslaw

Broccoli Walnut Salad

Phase 1 • Makes 6 to 8 servings   *Calories 215 – CARBS 23g • PROTEIN 6g • FAT 11g • FIBER 3g*

1 head	fresh broccoli (about 1 pound)
1 cup	red onion, chopped
½ cup	dark raisins
½ cup	walnuts
1 cup	red seedless grapes

DRESSING

½ cup	low-fat mayonnaise
½ cup	low-fat sour cream
1 tbsp	honey
½ tsp	ground ginger

1. Peel the tough outer skin from the broccoli stalk and discard. Chop the stalks into ½ inch pieces and cut the tops into small florets. (There should be about 6 cups of broccoli florets and stems).

2. In a large bowl, combine broccoli, onions, raisins, grapes and walnuts and toss well.

3. Dressing: In a small bowl, combine mayonnaise, sour cream, honey and ginger; stir to mix well. Add the dressing to the broccoli mixture and toss to mix.

4. Cover the salad and refrigerate for several hours or overnight before serving.

Nutrition Tip

Did you know? A handful of walnuts helps meet your daily requirement of omega-3 fatty acids. Eating a small handful each day will help to reduce the amount of LDL "bad" cholesterol in the blood. Walnuts are a source of protein, minerals, essential vitamins, and powerful antioxidants. Store walnuts in the refrigerator to avoid rancidity.

Colourful Black Bean and Corn Salad

Phase 2 • Makes 6 servings   *Calories 179 – CARBS 27g • PROTEIN 7g • FAT 6g • FIBER 7g*
This salad is best made at least 4 to 6 hours ahead of time to allow the flavours to blend.
It keeps well in the refrigerator for up to 3 days.

SALAD

1 can (19 oz/540 ml)	black beans, rinsed and drained
1 can (12 oz/341 ml)	corn kernels, drained
1	large tomato, diced
1	green bell pepper, diced
1	small red onion, finely chopped
2 tbsp	fresh cilantro, chopped

DRESSING

¼ cup	lime juice (juice of 1 lime)
2 tbsp	red wine vinegar
2 tbsp	flaxseed oil
1 tsp	ground cumin
½ tsp	hot pepper sauce (optional)
to taste	salt and pepper

1. In a large bowl, combine beans, corn, tomatoes, peppers, onions and cilantro. Set aside.

2. Dressing: In a small bowl or glass jar, whisk together lime juice, vinegar, oil, cumin, hot pepper sauce (if using), salt and pepper to taste.

3. Pour dressing over salad. Garnish with cilantro.

For a speedy dressing, add ½ tsp cumin to ¼ cup bottled oil and vinegar salad dressing.

Colourful Black Bean
and Corn Salad

Salads

Chicken Caesar Salad

Phase 2 (Phase 1 without the croutons) • Makes 4 to 6 servings
Calories 282 – CARBS 17g • PROTEIN 32g • FAT 10g • FIBER 6g

CAESAR DRESSING

¾ cup	1% cottage cheese
½ cup	skim milk
2	cloves garlic, minced
¼ cup	lemon juice, freshly squeezed (juice of one lemon)
1½ tsp	dijon mustard
1 tsp	Worcestershire sauce
½ tsp	salt
½ tsp	black pepper, freshly ground
1 tbsp	olive oil
¼ cup	parmesan cheese, freshly grated

QUICK CROUTONS

2	slices whole wheat bread
2 tsp	olive oil
½ tsp	garlic powder
¼ tsp each	dried oregano, basil and thyme or ¾ tsp Italian Seasoning

SALAD

8 cups	romaine lettuce, torn (about 2 medium heads)
¼ cup	parmesan cheese, freshly grated

CHICKEN

2 cups	cooked chicken, chopped

continued next page

1. Prepare the dressing: In a food processor or blender, purée cottage cheese and milk until smooth. Blend in garlic, lemon juice, mustard, Worcestershire sauce, salt and pepper. Add olive oil and blend until thick and smooth. Add parmesan cheese and blend until just mixed. Cover and refrigerate for at least 1 hour or up to a day.

2. Prepare the croutons: Cut bread into cubes. In a glass pie plate, toss bread cubes with olive oil, garlic powder and Italian seasoning. Microwave, covered with a paper towel, on High, stopping twice to stir, for 3 to 4 minutes, or until crisp. Set aside to cool.

3. Prepare the salad: Place lettuce in a large salad bowl, pour in dressing and toss. Sprinkle with parmesan and croutons, toss lightly and serve immediately.

4. Top with cooked chicken (heated if desired).

Caesar salad must be eaten immediately after tossing or it goes limp. Prepare the lettuce ahead of time and keep it crisp in a plastic bag with a paper towel inside. Make the dressing ahead of time and keep it in the refrigerator until ready to toss with the salad.

> **Nutrition Tip**
> Olive oil is an excellent source of monounsaturated fat. This fat may help to lower the risk of heart disease because it reduces total cholesterol as well as the LDL "bad" cholesterol in the blood. Try replacing other fats such as butter or margarine with olive oil.

Salads

Chicken Caesar Salad

Big Batch Creamy Cole Slaw

Phase 1 • Makes 8 to 10 servings　　　*Calories 86 – CARBS 12g • PROTEIN 2g • FAT 4g • FIBER 2g*

½ cup	low-fat mayonnaise
½ cup	low-fat plain yogurt
2 tbsp	sugar or sweetener of choice
2	green onions, finely chopped
2 tsp	lemon juice
1 tbsp	white vinegar
1 tbsp	dijon mustard
¼ tsp	celery seed
¾ tsp	salt
¼ tsp	black pepper
5 cups	cabbage, shredded
3 cups	carrots, grated
½ cup	dried cranberries (optional)

1. In a large bowl, mix together mayonnaise, yogurt, sugar, onion, lemon juice, vinegar, mustard, celery seed, salt and pepper.

2. Add cabbage, carrots and cranberries. Stir well.

3. Chill 1 to 2 hours before serving.

Nutrition Tip

Many artificial sweeteners are much sweeter than sugar, therefore less is needed to sweeten foods. Splenda™ is the trade name for sucralose, one of the more prevalent artificial sweeteners. Many people with diabetes or those following a low-G.I. diet use artificial sweeteners because they do not affect blood sugar. If you have concerns about artificial sweeteners, you can find an excellent medical overview at www.fda.gov. If you prefer not to use artificial sweeteners, then fructose is a better alternative than sugar. The herbal sweetener, stevia, which can be found in health food stores is also a great choice.

Curried Chicken and Apple Salad

Phase 1 • Makes 8 servings   *Calories 168 – CARBS 14g • PROTEIN 19g • FAT 4g • FIBER 1g*

This is Cheryl's teenage son Aaron's favorite recipe!

1 tbsp	canola oil
1 tbsp	curry powder
⅓ cup	purple onion, diced
2 tbsp	lemon juice, fresh
2 tbsp	sugar or sweetener of choice
¼ tsp	salt
⅓ cup	low-fat mayonnaise
⅓ cup	low-fat plain yogurt
2	cooked chicken breasts, cubed
3 stalks	celery, thinly sliced
½ cup	red bell pepper, chopped
1	medium apple, cut in ¼-inch cubes
6	dried apricots, diced
	salad greens

1. Dressing: Heat oil in a small saucepan over medium-high heat. Add curry powder and onion. Sauté 1 to 2 minutes or until onions are tender. Add lemon juice, sugar and salt. Simmer over medium heat until sauce begins to thicken, about 1 minute. Remove from heat and cool. Stir mayonnaise and yogurt into cooled sauce; set aside.

2. In a large bowl, toss together chicken, celery, red pepper, apple and apricots. Add dressing and gently toss until evenly coated.

3. Serve chicken mixture on a bed of salad greens. Garnish with chopped apricots and red pepper, if desired.

Salads

Curried Chicken and Apple Salad

Spinach Salad with Pears and Glazed Pecans

Phase 1 • Makes 8 servings   *Calories 255 – CARBS 12g • PROTEIN 30g • FAT 10g • FIBER 3g*

4	chicken breasts, cut into strips
9 cups	spinach leaves (or combination mixed greens)
2	med. ripe pears, cored and diced
1/3 cup	feta, crumbled

DRESSING

2 tbsp	orange juice concentrate, thawed
2 tbsp	olive oil
1 tbsp	balsamic vinegar
1 tsp	garlic, minced
½ tsp	honey
½ tsp	dijon mustard

Glazed Pecans (use only ½ cup for this recipe)

2 tbsp	sugar
¼ tsp	cinnamon
1/8 tsp	allspice
1/8 tsp	nutmeg
1 cup	pecans

1. Grill or stir-fry chicken strips, set aside. (or use quick prep chicken page 13)

2. In large bowl, combine spinach and /or mixed greens, pears and feta cheese. Set aside.

3. Dressing: Whisk orange juice concentrate, oil, balsamic vinegar, garlic, honey and mustard together in small bowl. Set aside.

4. Glazed pecans: mix sugar, cinnamon, allspice and nutmeg in a small bowl. Add pecans and mix well. In non-stick fry pan, on medium heat, sauté pecan mixture. Stir constantly until sugar is dissolved and nuts are glazed. Remove from heat when done. Let cool. (Note: this recipe uses only ½ cup of pecans; reserve remainder in airtight container for future use)

5. Toss spinach mixture with dressing, chicken, pecans and serve.

Spinach Salad with Pears and Glazed Pecans

Kidney Bean, Cabbage and Feta Salad

Phase 1 • Makes 6 servings   *Calories 138 – CARBS 19g • PROTEIN 7g • FAT 5g • FIBER 7g*

1 can (19 oz/540 ml)	red kidney beans, rinsed and drained
3 cups	cabbage, finely chopped
1	red bell pepper, chopped
2	green onions, chopped
½ cup	feta cheese, cubed
3 tbsp	fresh parsley, chopped

DRESSING

2 tbsp	lemon juice
1 tbsp	flaxseed oil
2	cloves garlic, minced
1 tsp	dried basil, optional

1. In a salad bowl, combine beans, cabbage, red pepper, onions, feta cheese and parsley.

2. In a jar with a tight fitting lid, combine dressing ingredients and shake.

3. Pour dressing over salad and toss lightly.

4. Cover and refrigerate until chilled.

Salads

Kidney Bean, Cabbage and Feta Salad

Lentil Rice Salad

Phase 2 • Makes 6 servings   *Calories 183 – CARBS 25g • PROTEIN 5g • FAT 7g • FIBER 3.5g*

½ cup	basmati rice
1 tbsp	olive oil
2	carrots, peeled, finely chopped
1	small onion, chopped
2 cloves	garlic, finely chopped
½ cup	dried green or brown lentils, rinsed and drained
1 cup	water or broth
1	red bell pepper, chopped

1. Cook rice according to package directions to yield 2 cups of cooked rice (½ cup raw).

2. Heat oil in a large saucepan. Add the carrot, onion and garlic and sauté until the onion is translucent, about 5 minutes. Stir in the lentils. Add water (or broth) and bring to a boil over high heat. Reduce heat and simmer for 20 to 25 minutes until lentils are tender but not mushy. Transfer the lentils to a large bowl.

3. Add red pepper and cooked rice to lentils. Toss with Lemon Basil Vinaigrette. Serve warm or chilled.

LEMON BASIL VINAIGRETTE

2 tbsp	flaxseed oil or olive oil
1 tsp	lemon rind, finely grated
¼ cup	lemon juice, freshly squeezed (juice of one lemon)
1½ tsp	fresh basil or ½ tsp dried basil
¼ tsp	salt

In a screw-top jar combine flaxseed oil, lemon rind, lemon juice, basil and salt. Cover and shake well.

Lentil Rice Salad

Mixed Bean Salad

Phase 1 • Makes 6 servings   *Calories 242 – CARBS 37g • PROTEIN 10g • FAT 6g • FIBER 11g*

Packed with fiber, this low-glycemic salad is perfect for lunch.

1 cup	green beans or 1 can (10 oz/284 ml), drained
1 cup	yellow beans or 1 can (10 oz/284 ml), drained
1 can (19 oz/540 ml)	chickpeas, drained
1 can (19 oz/540 ml)	red kidney beans, drained
1	small red bell pepper, chopped
½ cup	red onion, diced
¼ cup	fresh parsley, chopped
2 cups	romaine lettuce, shredded (optional)
2 cups	baby spinach leaves (optional)

DRESSING

⅓ cup	red wine vinegar
2 tbsp	flaxseed oil
1 tsp	sugar
2 cloves	garlic, minced
1 tbsp	Dijon mustard
2 tsp	celery seed
¼ tsp each	salt and pepper

Nutrition Tip

Green beans are packed with nutrients! They are a great source of fat-soluble vitamins (A, C, K), dietary fibre, potassium, folate, manganese, iron, and a number of other minerals.

Salads

1. If fresh green or yellow beans are being used, steam for about 5 minutes until tender crisp. Rinse under cold water until cool. Drain well. Cut in 1 inch pieces.

2. In a large bowl, combine steamed beans, canned beans, red pepper, onion and parsley.

3. To make dressing, combine red wine vinegar, flaxseed oil, garlic, dijon mustard, celery seed, salt and pepper in a jar with a tight lid. Shake well.

4. Pour over salad and toss gently.

5. Combine romaine and spinach and divide among 4 plates. Spoon bean mixture over greens to serve.

Mixed Bean Salad

Tabouli

Phase 1 • Makes 6 servings   *Calories 246 – CARBS 43g • PROTEIN 8g • FAT 6g • FIBER 10g*

Tastiest when fresh mint is available. Bulgur wheat is now universally available in bulk or prepackaged at your local grocery store. Add more vegetables as desired

1 cup	bulgur wheat
2 cups	boiling water
1 can (19 oz/540 ml)	chickpeas, drained and rinsed
1 cup	fresh parsley, chopped
½ cup	fresh mint, chopped
2	green onions, chopped
1 or 2	medium tomatoes, cut into small pieces

DRESSING

2 tbsp	flaxseed oil
1	lemon, juice and grated rind
1 tsp	salt
to taste	pepper

1. Measure bulgur wheat into a bowl and cover with boiling water. Let stand for ½ hour until all the water has been absorbed. Drain any excess and pat dry with a paper towel if necessary.

2. Stir chickpeas, parsley, mint, onions and tomatoes into bulgur.

3. Dressing: In a small bowl, whisk oil, lemon juice, lemon rind, salt and pepper. Pour over salad and mix well.

4. Chill for at least one hour before serving.

Covered and chilled, this dish will keep up to 4 days.

Colene's Spicy Carrot and Chickpea Salad

Phase 1 • Makes 6 servings   *Calories 204 – CARBS 33g • PROTEIN 6g • FAT 6g • FIBER 7g*

⅓ cup	low-fat plain yogurt
2 tbsp	olive oil
2 tbsp	lemon juice
½ tsp	sugar
1 tsp	ground cumin
½ tsp	ground coriander
¼ tsp each	salt and pepper
pinch	cinnamon and ginger
4 cups	carrots, grated
1 can (19 oz/540 ml)	chickpeas, rinsed and drained
2 tbsp	raisins or currants
2 tbsp	parsley, chopped
2 tbsp	fresh cilantro

Nutrition Tip

When choosing vegetables think orange, green and red. The colour is a reflection of its content of beta-carotene, a powerful antioxidant that protects against free radical damage. Carrots, broccoli, sweet potato, winter squash, and spinach are excellent sources of beta-carotene.

Salads

1. In a medium sized bowl, combine yogurt, oil, lemon juice, sugar, cumin, coriander, salt, pepper, cinnamon and ginger and mix well.

2. Add carrots, chickpeas, raisins, parsley and cilantro. Mix well.

3. Chill well before serving.

Colene's Spicy Carrot and Chickpea Salad

Quinoa and Black Bean Salad

Phase 2 • Makes 8 to 10 servings   *Calories 264 – CARBS 40g • PROTEIN 10g • FAT 8g • FIBER 7g*

Party favourite

1 cup	quinoa
1¼ cups	water
2 tbsp	olive oil
1	large onion, finely chopped (2 cups)
2 cloves	garlic, minced
1 tsp	paprika
1½ tsp	ground cumin
1½ tsp	ground coriander
2	red bell peppers, diced
¼ tsp	hot pepper flakes
1 tbsp	cilantro, chopped (optional)
1 can (12 oz/341 ml)	corn, drained
1 can (14 oz/398 ml)	black beans, drained
1	large tomato, diced
½ cup	feta cheese, crumbled
1 small can	black olives (optional)
½ cup	pine nuts, toasted (optional)
¼ cup	lemon juice, freshly squeezed (juice of one lemon)
to taste	salt and pepper

1. Combine quinoa and water in a saucepan. Cover and bring to a boil. Turn off heat and let sit 10 to 15 minutes, or until the water is absorbed. If you prefer quinoa with a firmer texture, use 1 cup of water.

2. Heat 1 tbsp oil in a frying pan. Sauté onion, garlic, paprika, cumin and coriander until onions are translucent. Stir in red bell peppers, hot pepper flakes and cilantro. Sauté another 5 minutes.

3. Add cooked quinoa to sautéed vegetables. Stir in the corn, black beans, tomato, feta, olives, pine nuts, lemon juice, salt and pepper. Transfer to a bowl and refrigerate until ready to serve.

Tip

Quinoa is a wonderful quick-prep food. Prepare ahead and have ready for salads and side dishes.

Greek Style Bulgur Salad

Phase 2 • Makes 4 to 6 servings   *Calories 209 – CARBS 28g • PROTEIN 7g • FAT 9g • FIBER 7g*

1 cup	bulgur wheat
2 cups	water
½	red onion, cut into rings
1	tomato, seeded and diced
1	green pepper, chopped
1	small zucchini, thinly sliced
½ cup	feta cheese
¼ cup	white wine vinegar
2 tbsp	flaxseed or olive oil
1 clove	garlic, minced
1 tsp	dried basil
1 tsp	dried oregano
1 tsp	salt
to taste	pepper

Salads

1. Boil water. Pour over bulgur and let stand for 30 minutes. Drain any excess water.

2. In a medium bowl, combine bulgur, onion, tomato, green pepper, zucchini and feta cheese.

3. In a separate bowl, combine vinegar, oil, garlic, basil, oregano, salt and pepper.
   Cover and refrigerate to allow flavours to develop.

To make this a Phase 1 recipe, eliminate the bulgur.

Bean Tortilla Pie *recipe page 90*

Main Meals

Szechuan Orange Ginger Chicken

Phase 1 • Makes 6 servings   *Calories 200 – CARBS 6g • PROTEIN 26g • FAT 8g • FIBER 1g*

1	orange, juice and grated rind
2 cloves	garlic, finely chopped
1 tbsp	fresh ginger, finely chopped
1 tbsp	cider vinegar
½ tsp	hot pepper sauce
1 tsp	sugar
1 tsp	cornstarch
2 tbsp	vegetable oil
3	chicken breasts
1	green bell pepper, cut into thin 1-inch strips
1	red bell pepper, cut into thin 1-inch strips

Nutrition Tip

Getting enough protein is critical for maintaining lean body mass, muscular strength, and a strong immune system. In addition to meat sources, choose protein-rich alternatives like dried beans, lentils, soy foods, and eggs more often. Including a protein at each meal and snack, will help control blood sugar, stave off hunger and keep you feeling full and satisfied.

1. Mix orange rind with chopped garlic and ginger and set aside.

2. Squeeze juice from orange and whisk together with vinegar, hot pepper sauce, sugar and cornstarch. Set aside.

3. Remove skin and bone from the chicken and slice into thin strips.

4. In a wok or large frying pan, heat the oil over medium-high heat. Cook the chicken in the hot oil for 3 to 4 minutes until cooked through or no longer pink inside. Remove chicken and set aside.

5. Cook the ginger, orange rind and garlic in the hot oil for 10 seconds. Add the bell peppers and stir-fry for
2 to 3 minutes.

6. Return the chicken and sauce to the stir-fry and cook until thickened.

For Phase 2, serve over cooked rice.

Main Meals

West Coast Teriyaki Salmon with Wasabi Mayonnaise

Phase 1 • Makes 4 servings   *Calories 304 – CARBS 15g • PROTEIN 25g • FAT 16g • FIBER 3g*

Prize Winning Recipe

4	salmon fillets (4 oz/125g each), skinless and boneless
½ cup	teriyaki marinade (recipe below) or store-bought equivalent
½ cup	sesame seeds, toasted

TERIYAKI MARINADE

½ cup	orange juice
3 tbsp	low-sodium soy sauce
2 tbsp	brown sugar
2 cloves	garlic, chopped
1½ tbsp	ground ginger (or 2 tsp fresh ginger, grated)

WASABI MAYONNAISE

1 tsp	water
½ tbsp	wasabi powder
¼ cup	low-fat mayonnaise
1 tbsp	onion, finely chopped

1. Rinse fish and place in shallow dish, coat with teriyaki sauce; set aside.

2. Preheat oven to 400°F.

3. In a small bowl, combine wasabi powder and water to create a paste. Let sit 1 minute, then combine with mayonnaise.

4. Remove salmon from marinade and discard marinade. Coat top and sides of fish with toasted sesame seeds. Place on a lightly oiled cookie sheet. Barbecue or bake for 15 minutes until fish is opaque and cooked through.

5. Serve with Wasabi Mayonnaise.

West Coast Teriyaki Salmon

"Old Fashioned" Hearty Beef Stew

Phase 2 • Makes 8 to 10 servings   *Calories 265 – CARBS 17g • PROTEIN 22g • FAT 12g • FIBER 4g*

2 tbsp	olive oil
2 lbs	stewing beef, cut into ½ inch cubes
2 cloves	garlic, minced
2	medium onions, chopped
2 cups	beef stock
3	medium carrots, peeled and cut in ¼ inch coins
3 stalks	celery, chopped
3	small red potatoes, peeled and sliced
1 can (19 oz/540 ml)	diced tomatoes with juice
1	bay leaf
1 tbsp	Worcestershire sauce
¼ cup	fresh parsley (or 2 tbsp dried)
1 cup	frozen peas
to taste	salt and pepper

Nutrition Tip

The richest sources of iron are from beef, poultry, pork and lamb. The type of iron in these sources can be absorbed most efficiently by the body. Iron from plant foods such as dried fruit, whole grains, leafy green vegetables, nuts, seeds and legumes are not well absorbed by the body. To improve their absorption, add a source of vitamin C to your meal, for example, spinach salad tossed with orange segments.

1. Heat oil in a large frying pan over medium heat. Add beef, garlic and onions and brown for about 5 minutes. Remove from heat and place mixture in a slow cooker.

2. Add stock, carrots, celery, potatoes, tomatoes (with juice), bay leaf, Worcestershire sauce and parsley; stir to combine. Cover and cook on Low for 8 to 10 hours or on high for 4 to 6 hours, until vegetables are tender and stew is bubbling. Remove bay leaf and discard.

3. Add peas 20 minutes before serving. Cook on high until slightly thickened and peas are heated through. Season to taste with salt and pepper.

Main Meals

"Old Fashioned" Hearty Beef Stew

Halibut in White Wine

Phase 1 • Makes 6 to 8 servings   *Calories 174 – CARBS 6g • PROTEIN 24g • FAT 6g • FIBER 1g*

2 pounds/900 grams	halibut fillets, de-boned and skinned
⅓ cup	whole wheat flour
¼ tsp	salt
¼ tsp	black pepper, freshly ground
2 tbsp	olive oil
1	large onion, finely chopped
1	large carrot, finely chopped
¾ cup	white wine, vegetable stock or chicken stock
1 tbsp	dried parsley or a few sprigs of fresh

1. Preheat oven to 375°F.

2. Wash halibut in cool water and pat dry.

3. Combine flour, salt and pepper in large bowl. Dredge all sides of halibut in flour mixture and set aside.

4. Heat 1 tbsp of the oil in a large frying pan. Brown halibut fillets on both sides, approximately 4 minutes per side. Place in oven proof dish.

5. Heat 1 tbsp of the oil in frying pan and sauté carrots and onions for about 5 minutes. Add wine or stock and simmer for another 5 minutes. Pour over fish. Sprinkle with freshly ground pepper.

6. Bake 25 minutes. Serve garnished with parsley.

Halibut in White Wine

Beef and Broccoli Stir-Fry

Phase 1 • Makes 4 servings   *Calories 203 – CARBS 8g • PROTEIN 18g • FAT 11g • FIBER 2g*

¾ pound/300 grams	beef, thinly sliced (use round or sirloin)
2 to 3 cups	broccoli, cut into bite-sized pieces
1 to 2 tbsp	oil
1 tbsp	fresh ginger, finely chopped
3 cloves	garlic, finely chopped

MARINADE

1 tbsp	soy sauce
1 tsp	water
1 tsp	sesame oil (optional)

SAUCE

⅓ cup	stock or water
1 to 2 tbsp	soy sauce
½ tsp	sugar
1 tbsp	cornstarch

Nutrition Tip

Milk products are not the only source of calcium. Broccoli is a source of calcium, as are beans, tofu, kale, sesame seeds, almonds, canned fish, and fortified rice and soy beverages.

1. Marinade: Whisk together the sauce, water and sesame oil. Toss with beef strips to coat. Refrigerate.

2. Sauce: Whisk together stock, soy sauce, sugar and cornstarch. Set aside.

3. In a wok or large frying pan, heat the oil over medium-high heat. Swirl gently to coat the sides of the pan. Cook the ginger and garlic in hot oil for 10 seconds.

4. Add the beef and stir-fry 2 to 3 minutes until almost cooked through. Add broccoli and continue to stir-fry for 5 to 7 minutes.

5. Add the sauce and continue to stir-fry until thickened.

Main Meals

Fish Fillets on Spinach

Phase 1 • Makes 6 servings   *Calories 172 – CARBS 6g • PROTEIN 23g • FAT 6g • FIBER 2g*

1½ pounds/600 grams	fish fillets (approximately 6 fillets)
¼ cup	lemon juice (juice of one lemon)
6 cups	fresh spinach
2 tbsp	olive oil
1	medium onion, chopped
1 tsp	salt
¼ tsp	black pepper
½ tsp	nutmeg
2	tomatoes, sliced
¼ cup	low-fat mozzarella cheese, grated

1. Preheat oven to 350°F.

2. Wash fish, pat dry. Sprinkle with lemon juice and let stand 10 minutes.

3. Heat oil in frying pan. Add onion and sauté until soft. Fry fish in pan with onions for a few minutes on each side until browned. Remove from frying pan and set aside.

4. Add spinach to frying pan and stir-fry 4 to 5 minutes.

5. Lightly oil a casserole dish and place spinach on the bottom. Arrange fillets on top of spinach. Place sliced tomatoes on top of fillets. Sprinkle salt, pepper, and nutmeg on tomato slices. Top with cheese.

6. Bake 15 minutes.

Fish Fillets on Spinach

Kidney Bean Curry (Raj Mah Di Dal)

Phase 2 • Makes 4 servings   *Calories 300 – CARBS 48g • PROTEIN 10g • FAT 8g • FIBER 9g*

2 tbsp	olive oil
1	small onion, chopped
4 cloves	garlic, diced
3 tsp	fresh ginger, diced
½ tsp	salt
1 tbsp	turmeric powder
½ tsp	ground coriander
to taste	cayenne pepper
1 can (19 oz/540 ml)	kidney beans
½ can	water
2 cups	cooked basmati rice

Nutrition Tip

Kidney beans are an excellent source of both soluble and insoluble fiber, containing 6 grams per ½ cup serving. Most people get only half of the 25 to 30 grams of fiber they need daily. Children need an amount of fiber that equals their age plus 5 grams.

1. Sauté onions in olive oil until slightly brown.

2. Add garlic and ginger and continue to sauté until browned.

3. Add salt, cayenne, turmeric, coriander, kidney beans and water. Bring to a boil and cook 10 to 12 minutes.

4. Serve over rice.

Meatless

Spaghetti Squash au Gratin

Phase 1 • Makes 6 servings   *Calories 142 – CARBS 12g • PROTEIN 10g • FAT 6g • FIBER 2g*

1	medium to large spaghetti squash
½ cup	parmesan cheese, grated
½ cup	mozzarella cheese, grated
⅓ cup	fresh parsley, chopped
1 tsp	oregano
2	Italian plum tomatoes, chopped

1. Pierce spaghetti squash several times with a fork or sharp knife (this will allow steam to escape during cooking). Microwave 10 to 12 minutes on high until shell is just soft, turning over half way through cooking. Remove and cool.

2. Preheat oven to 375°F.

3. Cut squash in half; remove and discard seeds. Use a fork to scrape insides of squash into a mixing bowl and separate strands. Reserve squash shells.

4. Toss squash strands and remaining ingredients together and spoon back into squash shell.

5. Bake 10 minutes or until lightly browned.

Spaghetti Squash au Gratin

Roasted Vegetables

Phase 1 • Makes 6 servings   *Calories 151 – CARBS 26g • PROTEIN 2g • FAT 5g • FIBER 5g*

5	large carrots, sliced into fries
3	sweet potatoes, sliced into fries
2	red bell peppers, quartered
1	large sweet onion, quartered
3 cloves	garlic, peeled
1 tsp	oregano
½ tsp each	salt and pepper
2 tbsp	olive oil

1. Position racks in top and bottom thirds of oven. Preheat to 450°F. Place two large rimmed baking sheets in oven while preheating.*

2. Toss all ingredients in a large bowl until vegetables are evenly coated with oil.

3. Remove baking sheets from oven, tumble vegetables onto sheets, and spread evenly.
   Roast 25 to 35 minutes, switching trays half way through roasting.

 * Heating baking sheets before adding vegetables seals in the flavour and helps vegetables develop a golden colour.

Roasted vegetables can be eaten as a side dish or used in Creamy Roasted Vegetable Soup on page 54.

Homemade Sweet Potato Fries

Phase 1 • Makes 6 servings.   *Calories 112 – CARBS 16g • PROTEIN 1g • FAT 5g • FIBER 2g*

3	medium sweet potatoes or yams, sliced into fries or wedges
2 tbsp	olive oil
1 tbsp	paprika
	seasonings of choice (oregano/basil)
to taste	salt and pepper

1. Preheat oven to 400°F.

2. Wash and peel sweet potatoes (or leave the skin on if desired). Toss in a large bowl with olive oil, paprika and spices until evenly coated.

3. Spread oiled fries on a baking sheet and bake for 15 minutes on one side.
   Turn over and bake 15 minutes on the other side. If desired, crisp further by putting under broiler for 2 to 3 minutes.

Barley Mushroom Pilaf

Phase 2 • Makes 6 to 8 servings   *Calories 146 – CARBS 24g • PROTEIN 8g • FAT 2g • FIBER 5g*

½ cup	fresh mushrooms, sliced
2 tsp	olive oil
1 cup	pearl barley
3 cups	beef broth
2	green onions, chopped
¼ tsp	ground savory
2 tbsp	parmesan cheese, grated

1. Heat olive oil in a saucepan; add mushrooms and sauté until soft.

2. Add barley, broth, green onion and savory. Bring to a boil. Reduce heat to low; cover and cook 45 minutes or until barley is tender and liquid is absorbed.

3. Sprinkle parmesan cheese over pilaf and serve.

Nutrition Tip

Barley is a chewy, versatile grain that is wonderful in soups and stews. It is one of the creamiest of all grains, and makes a delicious creamy pudding similar to rice pudding. Pot barley has only the outer husk removed. Pearl barley has had the bran removed and has been steamed and polished. Barley has a low glycemic index and can be used instead of rice.

Quinoa Pilaf

Phase 1 • Makes 6 servings   *Calories 190 – CARBS 30g • PROTEIN 7g • FAT 5g • FIBER 4g*

1 cup	quinoa
1½ cups	water
2 tbsp	olive oil
2 cloves	garlic, crushed
2 to 3 cups	vegetables, sliced (celery, green onion, green and red bell pepper, carrots, broccoli, cauliflower or zucchini)
2 tbsp	soy sauce or seasonings of choice (i.e. oregano, basil)
½ cup	toasted almonds (optional)

1. In a sieve, rinse quinoa under running water and drain.

2. In a medium saucepan or rice cooker, add water and quinoa. Cover and bring to a boil. Reduce heat and simmer 15 minutes or until tender. Use less water (1 cup) if you prefer quinoa with a firmer, chewier texture.

3. In a non-stick frying pan over medium heat, sauté garlic then stir-fry vegetables for about 4 minutes until tender crisp. Add cooked quinoa to vegetables. Add soy sauce or choice of seasonings.

4. Serve sprinkled with toasted almonds if desired.

Nutrition Tip

Quinoa (pronounced keen-wa) is a gluten free, low-glycemic grain with ancient origins. It comes from the Andes Mountains of South America, and was a staple in the Inca civilization. Quinoa is higher in protein than any other grain and a glycemic index of 35 makes it a great staple in your pantry. Quinoa is versatile, quick to prepare, and can be substituted for almost any grain in most recipes. Include generous amounts of grains in your diet and experiment with new ones, such as quinoa, bulgur, and buckwheat.

Meatless

Anya's Chickpea Burgers

Phase 1 • Makes 6 servings　　　　　*Calories 275 – CARBS 30g • PROTEIN 8g • FAT 14g • FIBER 6g*

Laura's daughter Anya, who has type 1 diabetes, loves these low-glycemic burgers.
Makes a great after school snack.

1 tbsp	olive oil
1	large onion, finely chopped
2 cloves	garlic, minced
1 can (19 oz/540 ml)	chickpeas, rinsed and drained
1 cup	whole grain bread crumbs, loosely packed
1	egg
¼ cup	flaxseed, ground
1 tsp	ground cumin
¼ tsp	salt
½ tbsp	dried parsley
pinch	cayenne pepper
1 to 2 tbsp	whole wheat flour (optional)

1. Heat oil in a frying pan. Add onion and garlic and cook over low heat for 5 minutes or until golden.

2. In a food processor, purée chickpeas until they resemble bread crumbs. Add bread crumbs, egg, flaxseed, cumin, salt, parsley, and pepper. Process for a few seconds.

3. Add onion and garlic mixture to ingredients in food processor. Process until just combined. Add whole wheat flour if mixture is too wet to form patties.

4. Form into patties.

5. Spray a non-stick frying pan with cooking spray and fry patties over medium heat until browned, approximately 4 minutes per side.

Delicious served with Greek salad.

Nutrition Tip

The chickpea, a legume also known as the garbanzo bean, is popular in Middle Eastern and Mediterranean dishes, including hummus and falafel. It is also a common ingredient in soups and salads. It has a low glycemic index, and is an excellent source of iron, protein and soluble and insoluble fibre.

Garden Vegetable Casserole with Rice

Phase 2 • Makes 4 to 6 servings   *Calories 279 – CARBS 35g • PROTEIN 20g • FAT 7g • FIBER 5g*

2 cups	cooked brown or basmati rice
2 cups	no-fat or 1% cottage cheese
2 tbsp	parmesan cheese, grated
1	medium onion, chopped
2	medium carrots, diced
1	medium green bell pepper, diced
3 cloves	garlic, finely chopped
1 tbsp	olive oil
1	medium zucchini, diced
1 can (19 oz/540 ml)	diced Italian tomatoes, drained
1 tbsp	dried oregano
1 tsp	salt
¼ tsp	black pepper
½ cup	low-fat mozzarella cheese, grated

Nutrition Tip

Zucchini is a dark green summer squash which resembles (in shape and size) a cucumber. The most tender and flavourful zucchini are young and no longer than 7 to 8 inches. They can be eaten raw or cooked in a variety of ways: fried, sautéed, broiled or grilled. Zucchini is a good source of folate, potassium and vitamin A.

1. Preheat over to 350°F.

2. Spread rice over the bottom of a lightly oiled 9 x 13 inch baking dish.

3. Mix the cottage cheese and parmesan cheese in bowl and spread over rice base.

4. In a large frying pan, sauté the onions, carrots, green pepper and garlic in oil until tender.

5. Add zucchini, diced tomatoes, oregano, salt and pepper to onion mixture. Reduce heat to simmer and cook covered for 5 minutes.

6. Spoon mixture over cottage cheese and top with grated mozzarella.

7. Bake 30 minutes or until bubbling.

Meatless

Lentil Spaghetti Sauce

Phase 1 • Makes 6 servings   *Calories 225 – CARBS 39g • PROTEIN 13g • FAT 2g • FIBER 11g*

1 tbsp	olive oil
1	large onion, chopped
2 stalks	celery, chopped
3 cloves	garlic, chopped
1¼ cups	dried red lentils, rinsed and drained
3 cups	water
1 can (19 oz/540 ml)	diced tomatoes with juice
2 cans (5.5 oz/156 ml)	tomato paste
2 tbsp	parsley, chopped
1 tsp	dried oregano
1 tsp	salt
¼ tsp	cayenne pepper
garnish	parmesan cheese, grated

1. Heat oil in a large pot over medium-high heat. Add onion, celery, and garlic and sauté for about 5 minutes, or until tender. Add lentils and water. Cover and cook on low for about ½ hour, or until lentils are tender. Stir often.

2. Add tomatoes, tomato paste and seasonings. Cook covered for about 15 minutes, or until lentils are soft and mushy. Add more water (up to 1 cup) if sauce becomes too thick.

3. Serve over cooked spaghetti squash (Phase 1) or spaghetti (Phase 2). Sprinkle with parmesan cheese.

Nutrition Tip

In addition to being a source of vitamin C, folate and potassium, tomatoes are also rich in a substance called "lycopene." Lycopene, found in higher quantities in cooked tomato products, is a powerful antioxidant that has been linked to a reduced incidence of cancer and heart disease.

Lentil Spaghetti Sauce

Roasted Yam Fajitas

Phase 2 • Makes 6 to 8 servings   *Calories 278 – CARBS 48g • PROTEIN 6g • FAT 8g • FIBER 6g*

6 or 8	whole wheat tortillas, 7- to 8-inch

FILLING

3	medium yams or sweet potatoes, peeled and cut into fries
2	carrots, julienned
1 each	medium red and green bell peppers, cut into strips
1	medium onion, sliced
2 tbsp	olive oil
to taste	salt and pepper

SAUCE

⅓ cup	orange juice
1 tsp	lime rind, grated
2 tbsp	lime juice (juice from one lime)
1 tbsp	olive oil
1 tbsp	garlic, minced
1 tsp	dried oregano
1 tsp	ground cumin
¼ tsp	hot pepper flakes

Nutrition Tip

Yam or sweet potato? Because of their similarities in size and shape, these two starchy vegetables are often thought to be related; however, they actually originate from two different species. Both have a lower glycemic index than potatoes and are packed with more beta-carotene.

1. Preheat oven to 350°F; place baking sheet in oven while preheating.

2. Filling: Toss yams, carrots, peppers and onion with oil. Place on baking sheet; sprinkle with salt and pepper to taste. Bake at 350°F for 20 to 25 minutes or until tender but not mushy.

3. Sauce: In a large bowl, combine orange juice, lime zest and juice, oil, garlic, oregano, cumin, hot pepper flakes. Add roasted vegetables and toss until coated.

4. Place vegetables in centre of tortillas and wrap.

Meatless

Sweet and Sour Tofu

Phase 1 • Makes 3 to 4 servings   *Calories 260 – CARBS 38g • PROTEIN 9g • FAT 8g • FIBER 4g*

1 tbsp	olive oil
1	onion, diced
2 cloves	garlic, minced
1 tbsp	fresh ginger, grated and peeled
2 or 3	carrots, sliced diagonally
1 each	green and red bell peppers, julienned
1 pkg (350 g)	extra firm tofu, drained and diced into 1 inch cubes
1 can (14 oz/398 ml)	pineapple chunks, drained (reserve juice)

SAUCE

	reserved pineapple juice
2 tbsp	brown sugar
¼ cup	vinegar
1 tbsp	cornstarch
2 tbsp	soy sauce

1. Mix sauce ingredients in a small bowl; set aside.

2. In a large frying pan over medium heat, sauté olive oil, onion, garlic and ginger for 5 minutes. Add carrots, peppers, tofu and pineapple.

3. Add sauce to frying pan. Bring to boil stirring constantly, then reduce heat and simmer for 2 to 3 minutes.

Nutrition Tip

Tofu is made from soy beans. Soy and ground flaxseed are the best dietary sources of phytoestrogens (isoflavones). Isoflavones have been shown to lower blood levels of bad cholesterol (LDL), increase good cholesterol (HDL), increase bone density and lower risk of breast cancer. 100 grams (3.5 oz) of tofu or 3 tablespoons of soy protein powder provide 75 mg of isoflavones, which is an excellent source towards your daily requirement.

Tofu Lasagna

Phase 1 • Makes 6 to 8 servings   *Calories 317 – CARBS 19g • PROTEIN 22g • FAT 17g • FIBER 5g*

"I can't believe there's no pasta!"

3 tbsp	extra virgin olive oil
1	zucchini, chopped
2	red bell peppers, chopped
1	medium onion, chopped
4 cloves	garlic, coarsely chopped
1 jar (24 oz/700 ml)	Italian tomato sauce
½ tsp each	dried oregano and dried basil
1 cup	mushrooms, sliced with stems removed
1 pkg (300 g)	soft tofu
1 pkg (300 g)	frozen spinach, drained
2 pkgs (350 g each)	extra firm tofu
1 cup	low-fat mozzarella cheese, grated
½ cup	parmesan cheese, grated

1. Preheat oven to 350°F.

2. In a frying pan over medium-high heat, add 2 tablespoons of the olive oil and sauté zucchini, peppers, onion and garlic until onions are transparent.

3. In a large bowl combine tomato sauce, oregano, basil, and mushrooms.

4. In another bowl, mix soft tofu with spinach.

5. Slice extra firm tofu into ⅛-inch to ¼-inch slices to act as lasagna noodles.

6. Oil a 9 x 13 inch lasagna pan with the remaining olive oil. Pour a thin layer of tomato sauce on the bottom. Add a layer of tofu as you would lasagna noodles. Top with some of the spinach mixture and then some grilled vegetables. Sprinkle some mozzarella on top.

7. Repeat until all ingredients are used (you will have 2 or 3 layers). Top with remaining mozzarella and lastly sprinkle with parmesan cheese.

8. Bake for 45 minutes to 1 hour.

Meatless

Tortilla Bean Pie *pictured on page 72*

Phase 2 • Makes 10 to 12 servings Calories 290 – CARBS 44g • PROTEIN 15g • FAT 8g • FIBER 10g

2 tbsp	olive oil
1 can (12 oz/341 ml)	corn kernels, drained
½	medium onion, chopped
2 cloves	garlic, minced
1	large red bell pepper, chopped
1 can (19 oz/540 ml)	kidney beans, rinsed and drained
1 can (19 oz/540 ml)	black beans, rinsed and drained
1 cup	Tomato Salsa (page 37) or store-bought equivalent
1 tsp	chili powder
1 tsp	ground cumin
1½ cups	low-fat cheddar cheese, grated
4	flaxseed tortillas, 8 inch

1. Preheat oven to 375°F. Spray an 8-inch springform pan with cooking spray.

2. In a medium saucepan, heat 1 teaspoon of the olive oil over medium heat. Add corn and cook until browned, 6 to 7 minutes. Remove corn and set aside.

3. In remaining oil, sauté onion, garlic and red bell pepper 6 to 7 minutes. Add corn and set aside.

4. Blend beans, salsa, chili powder, and cumin in a food processor or with a hand-held blender until smooth.

5. Place one tortilla in the bottom of an 8-inch spring-form pan. Top with a third of the bean mixture, then a third of the vegetable mixture, then a quarter of the cheese mixture.

6. Repeat layering of tortilla, bean, vegetables and cheese twice more. Top with last tortilla and remaining cheese.

7. Cover with foil and bake 40 to 45 minutes until heated through and cheese is melted.

8. Remove side of springform pan. Cut pie into wedges and serve.

Nutrition Tip

Black beans are a good source of soluble fiber and are low-glycemic, which causes a slow rise in blood sugar following a meal. Other good choices are chickpeas, navy beans, white beans, kidney beans and lentils.

Vegetarian Quiche with a Basmati Crust

Phase 2 • Makes 6 servings   *Calories 191 – CARBS 18g • PROTEIN 13g • FAT 8g • FIBER 2g*

CRUST

1½ cups	cooked basmati rice
2 tbsp	parmesan cheese, grated
1	egg white (reserve yolk for filling)

FILLING

5	eggs, beaten plus one yolk (remaining from crust ingredients)
1 cup	skim milk
2 tbsp	parmesan cheese, grated
1	red bell pepper, diced
1	medium zucchini, grated
¼ cup	fresh cilantro, chopped
½ cup	low-fat swiss or mozzarella cheese, grated
1 tbsp	Italian spice
½ tsp	black pepper
1	tomato, thinly sliced

Nutrition Tip

Rice, particularly sticky rice and regular white rice, tends to be higher glycemic than other grains. The lower glycemic rices include basmati (G.I. 58), parboiled (G.I. 38), long grain (G.I. 55). Choose these more often and keep serving sizes to ½ cup cooked.

1. Preheat oven to 350°F.

2. Crust: Mix together rice, parmesan cheese and egg white. Press into a 9-inch quiche pan or pie plate.

3. Filling: Mix eggs, milk, cheese, red bell pepper, zucchini, cilantro, cheese and spices and pour into crust. Layer tomato slices on top.

4. Bake 45 minutes.

5. Serve with salsa.

Meatless

Awesome Tofu Pizza

Phase 2 • Makes 3 servings   *Calories 200 – CARBS 8g • PROTEIN 16g • FAT 11g • FIBER 2g*

350 g	extra firm tofu
⅔ cups	chunky black bean salsa, fresh or store bought
¼ cup	black olives, pitted and coarsely chopped (optional)
2	green onions, thinly sliced
½ cup	grated cheddar
¼ cup	feta, crumbled
¼ tsp	dried oregano

1. Place oven rack in top third of oven. Preheat to 500°F.

2. Lightly grease a cookie sheet.

3. Turn tofu block on edge and slice into six thin slices. Place tofu slices on cookie sheet.

4. In a bowl, stir salsa with olives and green onion, then spoon over tofu and spread to edges. Sprinkle with cheddar, feta and oregano.

5. Turn oven to broil and cook until cheese melts, 6 to 8 minutes.

Spicy Dal with Chickpeas

Phase 1 • Makes 8 servings *Calories 205 – CARBS 30g • PROTEIN 10g • FAT 5g • FIBER 7g*

This dish is most flavourful if made ahead of time.

1 cup	dried red lentils, rinsed and drained
3 cups	vegetable stock or water
2 tbsp	canola oil
2 tsp	ground cumin
2 tsp	garlic purée (or 2 to 3 cloves put through a press)
1	onion, finely chopped
1 can (19 oz/540 ml)	chickpeas, rinsed and drained
1 tbsp	mild Indian curry paste
½ tsp	salt

> **Nutrition Tip**
> Some people avoid beans, peas and lentils because of the uncomfortable and potentially embarrassing consequences. When preparing your own beans, there are steps you can take to reduce gas (see below). Beano™ works well too.

1. In a medium pot, combine lentils with vegetable stock or water and bring to a boil. Cover, reduce heat and simmer for 15 minutes.

2. While the lentils are cooking, combine oil, cumin and garlic in a frying pan and sauté for 1 minute. Add the onion and continue to sauté for another 3 to 5 minutes, stirring constantly. Remove from heat and add to cooked lentils.

3. Add the chickpeas and stir in the curry paste and the salt.

For Phase 2, serve over rice.

PREPARING DRIED BEANS

Lentils, peas and beans are nutritious, versatile and easy to prepare. Lentils and split peas do not require soaking before cooking and are added dry to most recipes, whereas beans and whole peas need to be soaked before cooking.

For every cup of dried beans or whole peas, immerse in at least 3 cups of water. Let stand 12 hours. To reduce gas, add 1 tsp of baking soda to the soaking water.

For quick soaking, slowly bring dried beans and water to a boil and boil gently for 2 to 3 minutes. Remove from heat, add 1 tsp baking soda, and let stand from 1 to 4 hours.

To cook beans, discard soaking water and add 3 cups of fresh water for every cup of soaked beans. Simmer for 1½ to 2 hours or until tender. Using a pressure cooker will save time when cooking beans.

Meatless

Fruit Yogurt Parfait

Desserts & Snacks

Fruit Yogurt Parfait

Phase 2 • Makes 4 servings   *Calories 290 – CARBS 43g • PROTEIN 10g • FAT 10g • FIBER 5g*

2 cups	fresh or thawed unsweetened fruit, chopped (strawberries, raspberries, blueberries, cantaloupe, mango)
2 cups	low-fat, sugar-free yogurt, any flavour
1 cup	granola (see recipe below)

1. Evenly distribute half the granola into the bottom of four parfait dishes (⅛ cup per dish).

2. Add ½ cup of fruit to each dish, then ½ cup of yogurt per dish.

3. Garnish with remaining granola (approximately ⅛ cup per dish).

Granola with a Crunch

Phase 2 • Makes 16 servings of ¼ cup   *Calories 180 – CARBS 28g • PROTEIN 4g • FAT 7g • FIBER 3g*

3 cups	slow cook oats
1 cup	mixed nuts and seeds (sunflower seeds, sesame seeds, chopped walnuts, pecans, cashew or almonds
½ cup	dried, unsweetened shredded coconut
½ tsp or to taste	cinnamon
dash	salt
½ cup or to taste	maple syrup or honey
¾ cup	raisins or chopped dried fruit (optional)

1. Preheat oven to 350°F.

2. In a bowl, combine all ingredients except raisins.

3. Spread out on a rimmed baking sheet. Bake 30 minutes or a little longer, stirring occasionally. Mixture should brown evenly. For a crunchier granola, cook a little longer, taking care that it does not burn.

4. Remove from oven and add raisins or dried fruit. Cool, stirring occasionally until granola is room temperature.

Store in a sealed, air tight container.

Desserts

Apple Custard Crumble

Phase 2 • Makes 8 servings   *Calories 245 – CARBS 43g • PROTEIN 5g • FAT 8g • FIBER 4g*

8 cups	apples, sliced and peeled (about 8 apples)
¼ cup	sugar
2 tbsp	all-purpose flour
1 tsp	cinnamon
2	eggs
1 cup	milk
1 tsp	vanilla
1	lemon, grated rind only

CRUMBLE TOPPING

⅔ cup	slow cook oats
½ cup	brown sugar
¼ cup	whole wheat or all-purpose flour
2 tsp	cinnamon
3 tbsp	non-hydrogenated margarine

1. Preheat oven to 350°F. Lightly spray a 9-inch square or 10-inch circular baking dish.

2. Layer apple slices in the dish. Press to flatten.

3. In a bowl, mix sugar, flour, and cinnamon, then whisk in eggs until frothy. Whisk in milk, lemon rind and vanilla. Pour over apples.

4. Crumble Topping: In a bowl, combine oats, brown sugar, flour and cinnamon. With fingers, mix in margarine until mixture is crumbly. Sprinkle over apple mixture.

5. Bake about 50 minutes or until apples are tender, custard is thickened and topping is golden. Serve warm or cold.

Nutrition Tip

Rolled oats are easily digestible and a good source of soluble fibre. Old-fashioned slow cooking oats or steel cut oats have the lowest G.I. rating because the grain is intact and has had minimal processing. Low G.I. means the carbohydrate is digested slowly and converted gradually to blood sugar, helping you feel full and energized longer after your meal. Choose slow cook oats more often!

Apple Custard Crumble

Low GI Brownies

Phase 2 • Makes 12 bars   *Calories 144 – CARBS 24g • PROTEIN 3g • FAT 5g • FIBER 2g*

3 ounces	semisweet or bittersweet chocolate
1 cup	carrot purée
½ cup	light or dark brown sugar, firmly packed
¼ cup	unsweetened cocoa powder
2 tbsp	trans-fat-free soft tub margarine spread
2 tsp	pure vanilla extract
2	large eggs
½ cup	white flour
½ cup	whole wheat flour
½ tsp	baking powder
½ tsp	salt

1. Make carrot purée by steaming 2 to 3 carrots until soft. Cool and blend to purée.

2. Preheat the oven to 350°F. Grease an 8x8 inch baking pan with non-stick cooking spray.

3. Melt the chocolate in a double boiler.

4. In a large bowl, combine melted chocolate, carrot purée, sugar, cocoa powder, margarine and vanilla. Whisk 1 to 2 minutes until smooth and creamy. Whisk in eggs.

5. Combine flour, baking powder and salt. Add to liquid mixture, stirring with a wooden spoon.

6. Pour batter into pan and bake 35 to 40 minutes. Cool completely in the pan before cutting into 12 bars. Sprinkle lightly with cocoa powder, or cocoa powder mixed with icing sugar.

Low GI Brownies

Ricotta Cheesecake

Phase 1 • Makes 14 servings   *Calories 130 – CARBS 8g • PROTEIN 8g • FAT 7g • FIBER 0g*

¼ cup	graham cracker crumbs
4 cups	ricotta cheese (two 500ml containers)
⅓ cup	sugar
3	large eggs
½ cup	low-fat yogurt
1 tsp	pure vanilla extract
1 tsp	lemon peel, finely grated
2 tbsp	cornstarch
1 tsp	baking powder

1. Preheat oven to 350°F. Sprinkle graham cracker crumbs in the bottom of a lightly sprayed 8-inch springform pan.

2. Cream ricotta and sugar until smooth. Add eggs, one at a time, and combine until blended. Add yogurt, vanilla and lemon peel and blend well.

3. Fold the cornstarch and baking powder into the mixture until combined.

4. Pour into pan and bake 50 to 55 minutes, or until tester comes out clean and cake is no longer loose. Chill.

5. Garnish with 1 cup fresh raspberries or raspberry purée if desired.

Nutrition Tip

Hard cheeses can still be eaten if moldy portions are cut off and discarded. However, if you discover mold in a soft cheese such as ricotta, cottage or brie, throw it out! The moisture in these cheeses makes it easy for microbes to infiltrate and contaminate the entire cheese.

Noel's Apple Bran Muffins

Phase 2 • Makes 12 muffins   *Calories 131 – CARBS 30g • PROTEIN 5g • FAT 2g • FIBER 5g*

¾ cup	All-Bran™ cereal
1 cup	skim milk
1	egg, lightly beaten
2 tsp	canola oil
½ cup	applesauce (unsweetened)
⅔ cup	whole wheat flour
⅓ cup	brown sugar
2 tsp	baking powder
½ tsp	baking soda
¼ tsp	salt
1 tsp	allspice
½ tsp	cloves
1½ cups	oat bran
⅔ cup	raisins
1	large apple, peeled and cut into ¼ inch cubes

1. Preheat oven to 350°F.

2. Mix the All-Bran™ and skim milk in a bowl and let stand for a few minutes.

3. In a small bowl, combine egg, oil and applesauce.

4. In a large bowl, mix flour, sugar, baking powder, baking soda, salt and spices. Stir in the oat bran, raisins and apple.

5. Add the All-Bran™ mixture and the applesauce mixture to the dry ingredients.

6. Spoon into an oil-sprayed 12-muffin pan. Bake 20 minutes or until lightly browned.

Noel's Apple Muffins

Peanut Butter Granola Bars

Phase 2 • Makes 60 small squares   *Calories 196 – CARBS 20g • PROTEIN 5g • FAT 11g • FIBER 3g*
This is a high energy bar that is great after workouts and sports.

1 cup	natural peanut butter
⅓ cup	brown sugar, tightly packed
½ cup	honey
⅓ cup	non-hydrogenated margarine
2 tsp	vanilla
3 cups	slow cook oats
½ cup	coconut
½ cup	sunflower seeds
½ cup	raisins
¼ cup	ground flaxseed
½ cup	almonds, sliced
½ cup	chocolate chips

1. Preheat oven to 350°F.

2. Cream peanut butter, brown sugar, honey, margarine and vanilla together until smooth.

3. Add oats, coconut, sunflower seeds, raisins, flax meal, almonds and chocolate chips. Mix well. Pat into oiled 13 x 9 baking dish.

4. Bake 20 to 25 minutes. Cool on a rack. Cut when cool.

Including Healthy Fats in Your Diet

- Cut back on the total amount of fat you consume and emphasize healthier fats such as olive oil, canola oil and flaxseed oil.
- Choose whole grains, vegetables and fruits more often.
- Choose fish, leaner cuts of meat and lower-fat dairy products.
- Limit your intake of fat from oils, spreads, sauces, desserts and greasy snack food.
- Read labels and avoid trans fat.

Fiber Feast Bread

Phase 2 • Makes 16 slices/servings   *Calories 108 – CARBS 23g • PROTEIN 4g • FAT 1g • FIBER 3g*

½ cup	boiling water
1 cup	raisins
1	egg, beaten
¼ cup	brown sugar
1 cup	buttermilk
1 cup	whole wheat flour
1 cup	slow cook oats
1 cup	100% bran cereal (such as All Bran™ or Fibre 1™)
¼ cup	wheat germ
1½ tsp	baking soda
½ tsp	salt

1. Preheat oven to 350°F. Lightly oil a loaf pan with non-stick spray.

2. In a large bowl, pour boiling water over raisins and let cool. Add egg, sugar and buttermilk.

3. In another bowl, combine flour, oats, bran cereal, wheat germ, soda and salt. Mix well.

4. Stir dry ingredients into raisin mixture until well blended. Pour into loaf pan.

5. Bake 45 to 50 minutes, or until loaf tests done.

Nutrition Tip

We need more fiber. It is estimated that people need twice as much fiber as they're getting now. Your intake should be at least 25 grams of fiber per day. Oats are an excellent source of soluble fiber which helps in the regulation of blood sugar and lowering blood cholesterol levels. Other good sources of soluble fiber include: oat bran, legumes (dried beans, peas and lentils), brown rice, barley and pectin rich fruit: apples, strawberries and citrus fruits.

Snacks

Mini Pita Fruit Snack

Phase 2 • Makes 1 serving   *Calories 86 – CARBS 13g • PROTEIN 4g • FAT 2g • FIBER 2g*

¼	apple or pear, chopped
pinch	cinnamon
1	mini whole wheat pita
2 tsp	low-fat cheddar or mozzarella cheese, grated

1. Cut slit in pita for opening.

2. Sprinkle chopped fruit with cinnamon.

3. Spoon fruit into top of pita. Top with cheese.

Tortilla Chips

Phase 2 • Makes 8 servings (1 serving is 8 chips)
Calories 187 – CARBS 26g • PROTEIN 5g • FAT 7g • FIBER 5g

8	8-inch flour tortillas, whole wheat, flax or multi-grain
1 tbsp	olive oil
to taste	seasoning of choice (Italian, garlic and chili, lemon and herb)

1. Preheat oven to 375°F.

2. Lightly brush olive oil on top of each tortilla. Stack 4 tortillas, then with kitchen scissors or a long knife, cut into eight wedges.

3. Place on a cookie sheet. Sprinkle with seasonings and parmesan cheese and bake for 15 minutes. Be careful not to over brown.

Tortilla chips will keep up to 2 weeks in an airtight plastic bag at room temperature.

Roasted Almonds

Phase 1 • 1 serving is 12 almonds)   *Calories 85 – CARBS 3g • PROTEIN 3g • FAT 7g • FIBER 1g*

Try this simple way to flavour raw almonds. They're great as salad toppings and snacks.

2 cups	raw almonds
1	egg white, beaten
to taste	various spices and flavourings, such as chili seasoning, cajun seasoning, sugar, cinnamon, spicy Dijon mustard

1. Preheat oven to 325°F.

2. Whip egg white in bowl with whisk; add almonds. Coat well and divide into 4 portions. Add spices to taste to make a variety of flavours.

3. To keep flavours separate, make aluminum foil trays by folding up the sides to resemble shoebox lids. Add flavoured nuts.

4. Bake 2 minutes.

> **Nutrition Tip**
>
> Almonds are a good source of calcium and iron. A snack of dried apricots and almonds provides carbohydrates, protein, fibre and iron. For convenience, prepackage apricots and almonds in snack-size zip-lock bags. Portioning out the snack ahead of time will help prevent you from eating too much.

Chickpea Snacks

Phase 1 • 1 serving is ¼ cup   *Calories 70 – CARBS 12g • PROTEIN 4g • FAT 1g • FIBER 2g*

2 cans (19 oz/540 ml)	chickpeas, drained and rinsed
1 tbsp	olive oil
1 tsp	salt
½ tsp	ground cumin
½ tsp	turmeric powder
½ tsp	ground coriander
½ tsp	chili powder
½ tsp	garlic powder

1. Preheat oven to 400°F.

2. In a large bowl or a large plastic bag, toss chickpeas with oil and spices. Spread onto large baking sheets in a single layer.

3. Bake 45 minutes to 1 hour, shaking a few times during baking. Chickpeas will be golden brown when done. Remove and let cool.

Store in a paper bag to keep fresh.

Snacks

Healthy Snacks

Keep it healthy, keep it handy

Nutrition Tip

Keep healthy snacks handy! It is important to keep your blood sugar relatively level by eating every 3 to 4 hours. You are less likely to grab an unhealthy snack if you avoid becoming overly hungry.

PHASE 1 SNACKS

- 6 celery sticks with 2 tablespoons low-fat cream cheese
- 1 sliced apple with 1 tablespoon peanut butter
- 1 sliced pear with 1 tablespoon soft goat cheese (20 % MF or less)
- 1 cup fresh fruit salad with 1 tablespoon sunflower seeds
- 4 dried apricot halves with 4 walnuts (or 6 almonds)
- 1 cup vegetable juice with 6 almonds
- 1 apple with low-fat cheese string
- 1 cup grapes with 6 plain almonds
- low-fat cheese string rolled up in 1 slice of deli meat (chicken, turkey, ham, beef; buy oven-roasted meats only, as most others are full of preservatives)
- ½ cup cottage cheese, ½ sliced banana, 1 teaspoon vanilla and sweetener of choice (optional)
- 1 cup heated skim milk, 1 teaspoon vanilla
- ½ cup Jello™ sugar-free pudding with ¼ cup slivered almonds
- ½ cup raw vegetables with 2 tablespoons Hummus (recipe page 39)
- frozen single-serve (no sugar added) yogurt
- fresh fruit kabob
- pickled asparagus rolled in slice of ham
- unsweetened applesauce with ¼ cup slivered almonds
- celery sticks with natural peanut butter and ⅛ cup raisins

PHASE 2 SNACKS

- all Phase 1 snacks
- 1 hard boiled egg with a Wasa™ cracker
- 2 low-glycemic crackers (i.e. Wasa™, Ryvita™) with 1 tablespoon peanut butter
- ½ can water packed tuna on cracker
- oven-roasted deli meats with 1 Wasa™ cracker and a pickle
- 6 to 8 homemade pita chips with salsa (recipe page 102)
- 1 muffin (recipe page 99) with 1 slice low-fat cheddar
- 1 cup coleslaw (recipe page 57) with 1 slice sprouted wheat bread

CARDIOVASCULAR DISEASE IN YOUTH

Studies are now showing us that children ages 10 to 18 have evidence of early "hardening of the arteries" or cardiovascular disease. This has been documented via ultrasound of their arteries. Childhood obesity is also at epidemic proportions, primarily due to the insulin resistance they are developing so early in life because of poor food choices and lack of exercise. This can be reversed through low-glycemic eating, more emphasis on fruits and vegetables, and 60 to 90 minutes of activity throughout the day.

Menu Planning

The following menu plan demonstrates how to incorporate recipes into a program for weight loss or management. Please note that if you have started your dietary changes with a five-day low-glycemic fibre cleanse, feel free to include extra vegetables, vegetable salads or a home made vegetable soup, such as Clean Sweep Soup on page 35, if you miss chewing or are hungry.

PHASE 1

As mentioned on page 11, Phase 1 eliminates breads, grains, rice, cereal, pasta, potatoes, sugar, candy, donuts, juices, and pop. This will help diminish carbohydrate cravings and reverse insulin resistance. All Phase 1 recipes on the following menu plans are interchangeable.

PHASE 2

This maintenance phase re-introduces some breads, rice, cereals, and potatoes that will not spike your blood sugar. These include carbohydrates with a lower glycemic index. Sugary treats, pop and junk food should be a rarity in any diet. Phase 2 allows you the freedom of substituting any recipe, Phase 1 or 2, for another.

How to portion your plate

TIPS FOR CONTINUED SUCCESS

- Eat at regular times.
- Choose a variety of foods from all food groups.
- Avoid or limit sugars and sweets.
- Reduce the amount of saturated and trans fats that you eat. Include more healthy fats (olive, canola and flaxseed oils).
- Include high fibre foods.
- Limit salt, alcohol and caffeine.
- Try something new! Low-glycemic choices such as barley, bulgur, lentils, or quinoa can help prevent boredom.
- When choosing a nutritional bar, look for one with a low glycemic rating.

Weight Loss Phase 1: One Week Sample Menu

- *For optimal nutrition, this meal plan should be complemented with a high quality nutritional supplement including calcium and vitamin D.*
- *To keep hydrated, drink 6 to 8 glasses of water daily.*
- *You can replace any meal with a low-glycemic shake.*

	Monday	Tuesday	Wednesday	Thursday	Friday	Saturday	Sunday
BREAKFAST	• Two-eggs scrambled plus ¼ cup Salsa page 37 • 1 apple	• Phase 1 low-glycemic shake of choice page 18	• ½ cup cottage cheese • 1 cup grapes • ½ orange	• Country Garden Omelette page 20 • ½ grapefruit	• Phase 1 low-glycemic shake of choice	• Egg and Tofu Scramble page 43	• ½ grapefruit • ¾ cup unsweetened yogurt • 6 almonds
SNACK	• ¼ cup chickpea snacks page 103 • 1 cup grapes	• ½ cup cottage cheese • ½ sliced banana • 1 tsp vanilla	• ½ cup raw veggies • 2 tbsp hummus page 39	• ½ cup broccoli florets • 2 tbsp Tzatziki page 39	• ½ cup cottage cheese • 1 cup grapes	• 6 celery sticks • 2 tbsp low-fat cream cheese	• 1 apple • 1 slice low-fat cheese
LUNCH	• Curried Chicken and Apple Salad page 63 • carrot sticks	• Mixed Bean Salad page 67	• Ground Beef Stroganoff leftovers	• Red Lentil Soup leftovers and Broccoli Walnut Salad page 58	• Szechuan Orange Ginger Chicken leftovers	• Kidney Bean, Cabbage and Feta Salad page 65	• Teriyaki Salmon and Vegetables leftovers
SNACK	• ½ cup raw veggies • 2 tbsp Tzatziki Sauce page 39	• 1 low fat cheesestring • 1 slice oven-roasted deli meat	• 1 cup fresh fruit salad • 2 tbsp slivered almonds	• 1 cup heated skim milk • 1 tsp vanilla • sweetener of choice	• 1 cup raw veggies • 2 tbsp tzatziki page 39	• 1 banana • 1 tbsp peanut butter	• 1 cup fresh fruit • ½ cup non-fat yogurt
DINNER	• Ground Beef Stroganoff page 27 • Basic Salad with Yogurt Dill Dressing page 55	• Red Lentil Soup page 50 • Salmon Waldorf Salad page 32	• Szechuan Orange Ginger Chicken page 73 • 1 cup steamed veggies	• Lettuce Wraps page 29 • Basic Salad page 55	• Colene's Spicy Carrot and Chickpea Salad page 69	• West Coast Teriyaki Salmon with Wasabi Mayo page 74 • Roasted Vegetables page 81	• Tofu Lasagna page 89 • Basic salad with Ginger-Sesame Dressing page 56
DESSERT	• 1 cup fresh berry medley	• 1 apple	• 1 kiwi fruit	• 2 fresh plums (small)	• 1 cup fresh pineapple • ½ cup yogurt	• Ricotta Cheesecake page 98	• 1 orange • ½ cup yogurt

Reminder: Phase I eliminates all sugars, breads, white flour, cereals, pasta, rice and potatoes (see page 21)

Maintenance Phase 2: One Week Sample Menu

- For optimal nutrition, this meal plan should be complemented with a high quality nutritional supplement including calcium and vitamin D.
- To keep hydrated, drink 6 to 8 glasses of water daily.
- You can replace any meal with a low-glycemic shake.

	Monday	Tuesday	Wednesday	Thursday	Friday	Saturday	Sunday
BREAKFAST	• Breakfast-on-the-run *page 20*	• Egg Tortilla Bowl *page 45* • ½ cup fresh fruit	• Phase 1 or 2 shake *pages 18 and 19*	• 1 egg, scrambled • 1 piece sprouted grain toast • ½ cup fruit • ½ cup yogurt	• Lemon Tart Smoothie *page 19*	• Flaxseed Pancakes with fresh fruit *page 41*	• French Toast *page 21* • ½ cup low-fat yogurt
SNACK	• 1 cup grapes • 6 plain almonds	• Noel's Apple Bran Muffin *page 99* • 1 slice low-fat cheese	• Noel's Apple Bran Muffin • 1 tbsp peanut butter	• 4 dried apricot halves • 4 walnuts	• 1 banana • chai tea	• 1 cup raw veggies • 2 tbsp Tzatziki *page 39*	• ½ cup cottage cheese • ¾ cup fresh berries
LUNCH	• Mix and Match Wrap of choice *page 34*	• Thai Chicken Tortilla Pizza leftovers • 1 apple	• Quinoa Salad leftovers	• Salmon Salad Fajitas with a sprouted grain tortilla *page 32* • Basic Salad with Orange Vinaigrette *page 55*	• Beef and Broccoli Stir-fry leftovers • ½ cup basmati rice	• Minestrone Soup leftovers • 2 Wasa crackers with 1 tbsp peanut butter	• Greek Style Bulgur Salad *page 71* • 1 apple
SNACK	• 10 baby carrots • 1 tbsp low-fat salad dressing	• 1 cup raw veggies • 2 tbsp Dip with a Twist *page 38*	• 1 apple • 1 slice low-fat cheese	• 2 Wasa crackers • 1 tbsp peanut butter	• 10 slices cucumber • 1 tbsp low-fat salad dressing	• 1 Low-G.I. Brownie *page 97*	• 2 Wasa crackers • 1 cheese string
DINNER	• Thai Chicken Tortilla Pizza *page 24* (make enough for leftovers!)	• Quinoa and Black Bean Salad *page 70* • Basic Salad with Ginger-Sesame Dressing *page 56*	• Beef and Broccoli Stir-fry *page 77* • ½ cup basmati or long-grain brown rice	• Vegetarian Quiche *page 91*	• Minestrone Soup *page 48* • 1 whole wheat pita, sliced and toasted with Big Batch Tomato Salsa *page 37*	• Halibut in White Wine *page 76* • 1 cup steamed veggies	• Cleansweep Stir-fry *page 35*
DESSERT	• Fruit Yogurt Parfait *page 95*	• ½ cup yogurt • 1 cup grapes • 2 tbsp Granola *page 95*	• 1 kiwi fruit • ½ cup low-fat yogurt	• 1 cup fresh fruit • 2 tbsp Fruit Dip *page 38*	• ½ cup yogurt • ¾ cup fresh berries	• 1 cup fresh fruit salad	• 1 cup fresh fruit • 2 tbsp Fruit Dip *page 38*

Reminder: Phase II introduces whole grain breads and cereals, pasta, low GI rice and pasta, and certain potatoes in moderation (see page 21)

ARE YOU EATING BECAUSE OF HUNGER?

Sometimes we use food to satisfy feelings other than hunger. The next time you are thinking about eating, take a moment to figure out if you are truly hungry. You might instead be experiencing emotions that are triggering your desire to eat. Say "HALT" out loud before you reach for a snack. HALT stands for "Hungry, Angry, Lonely or Tired. Which are you feeling? If it's not hunger, food is not the solution.

COMMON QUESTIONS

What should I do if carbohydrate cravings return?

Inevitably, you will at some time eat too many high-glycemic carbohydrates over a short period of time. This could happen on a vacation, during the holidays, or it may simply be the result of slipping into unhealthy eating patterns. It is important to recognize this situation quickly and get back on track. Otherwise, you will once again begin to get hungry and crave high-glycemic carbohydrates. When this happens it is wise to figure out what got you back into this pattern.

The best way to reduce this carbohydrate addiction is to return to Phase 1 of the *Heathy for Life* program. In Phase 1 you need to avoid all sugar, bread, flour, cereals, rice, pasta, and potatoes. The medical literature shows us that this is a critical time in any healthy lifestyle program, and failure to recognize these signs early can lead to a major setback. Once you have gained control of your cravings and your appetite is reduced, you can slowly return to Phase 2.

How do I order low-glycemic foods when eating in restaurants?

When eating out, plan in advance. Try to choose a restaurant that has a menu offering healthy choices such as grilled fish, meat and poultry dishes, and lots of fresh vegetables and salads. Keep in mind that portion sizes are usually larger than those at home. You need to be assertive and ask for your meal the way you want it. Here are some tips:

- Order a green salad with lots of vegetables to start with a low-fat dressing on the side so you can control the amount you use. Salads have a very low G.I. rating and will help you fill up before the main course arrives.
- Order an entrée with more emphasis on protein and vegetables. For example, a chicken and veggie stir-fry or a dinner size salad topped with grilled chicken, beef or fish are excellent choices.
- Avoid bread and starchy side dishes. Ask for a side salad instead of mashed potatoes, fries or rice.
- Instead of ordering one large entrée, order two appetizers, or an appetizer and a salad, as your meal.
- Consider sharing an entrée with a friend.
- Eat slowly. Your stomach can take up to 30 minutes to let your brain know you are full.
- Ask that the rice or potatoes be held and that the vegetables be doubled.

The Importance of Cellular Nutrition

For years, it was believed that people could get all the nutrients they needed from their diet. However, after researching the medical literature and working with physicians such as Dr. Ray Strand, it became apparent that every man, woman, and child needs to be taking nutritional supplements in order to better protect their health and minimize oxidative stress.

What is oxidative stress?
As the body utilizes the oxygen needed to sustain life, occasionally a charged oxygen molecule is produced called a free radical. If the free radical is not neutralized by an antioxidant, it can go on to create even more volatile free radicals. These highly reactive free radicals damage cell walls and vessels, proteins, fats and even the DNA nucleus of a cell.

Free radical damage is caused by:

- excessive emotional stress
- radiation from the sun
- cigarette smoke
- excessive exercise
- poor diet – high-glycemic and high-fat
- pollutants in our air, food and water
- medication
- elevated blood sugar (caused by type 1 or type 2 diabetes)

How can you minimize oxidative damage?
The best way is to ensure you have enough antioxidants available to handle the number of free radicals produced. If not, oxidative stress occurs and the body is vulnerable to degeneration similar to rust on a car. The body produces some antioxidants and we are able to get additional antioxidants from our food — primarily from fruits and vegetables.

Unfortunately, there is a a gap in our protection because our foods have become significantly depleted of antioxidants and supporting minerals as a result of mineral depletion in the soil, green harvesting and loss of nutrients through over processing and long transportation distances. The gap is widened further by our poor food choices and food preparation methods. Research has shown that the general population consumes significantly less than the recommended intake for calcium, vitamin D, chromium, selenium, copper, folic acid, vitamins B6 and B12, and vitamin E. Similarly, studies show that well over 50 percent of children do not get the daily recommended intakes (DRI) of many nutrients.

Oxidative stress has now been shown via medical research to be the root cause of over 70 chronic degenerative diseases, including heart disease, stroke, cancer, type 2 diabetes, arthritis, Alzheimer's dementia, macular degeneration, lupus, MS, and the list goes on.

What is the answer to oxidative stress and poor quality diets?
Nutritional supplements are the answer because it is difficult to get all the nutrients you need from your diet — even with healthy eating. Consider what you must eat to receive an optimal amount

of 400 IU of vitamin E, one of the most powerful antioxidants to combat free radicals: 33 pounds of spinach, 5.2 pounds of wheat germ, 2.2 pounds of almonds, or 1 quart of safflower oil!

CRITERIA FOR CHOOSING A GOOD QUALITY NUTRITIONAL SUPPLEMENT

Is it a pharmaceutical grade nutritional supplement?

The nutritional supplement industry is basically an unregulated industry. There is no guarantee that what is on the label is actually in the tablet. You need to select a company that manufactures their products according to pharmaceutical grade Good Manufacturing Practices (GMP). This means that they purchase pharmaceutical grade raw ingredients and then produce them with the same quality control as they would medications. You will be guaranteed that you are getting what you paid for.

Does it meet US Pharmacopoeia (USP)?

When the company follows USP guidelines, it gives you the assurance that your tablets will dissolve. Unfortunately, many supplements fall short and do not meet the USP.

Is your supplement complete and balanced?

According to Dr. Strand, supplements need to provide optimal levels of several different antioxidants and their supporting B co-factors (vitamins B1, B2, B5, B6, B12 and folic acid) along with the minerals selenium, magnesium, zinc, copper, manganese, chromium and vanadium. Your body needs these nutrients in the proper balance to create a synergy. Synergy means that the nutrients work together at the cellular level to enhance the body's natural immune system.

For more information on choosing a good quality supplement and which ones have the best ratings, check out Lyle MacWilliam's book *Nutrisearch Comparative Guide to Nutritional Supplements 4th edition,* which rates over 1500 U.S. and Canadian supplements. It is available at www.amazon.com.

Get Fit to Get Healthy

What if someone told you that a thinner, healthier, and longer life was within your grasp? Sound too good to be true? According to a wealth of research, exercise is the silver bullet for a better quality of life.

We know that being inactive has contributed greatly to our unhealthy society, to the point that we are increasing our risk of many chronic diseases including diabetes, hypertension, cardiovascular disease and many cancers. Other common problems include aching muscles and joints, back problems, fatigue and even psychological effects such as depression.

Finding activities that you enjoy and that become part of your daily routine is the key to a long and healthy life. The requirements are relatively simple – just do it.

HEALTH BENEFITS

- Weight management
- Fewer health problems
- Improved immune system
- Elevated moods
- Improved sleep patterns
- Stress reduction
- Improved balance
- Reduced blood pressure
- Lower LDL ("bad") cholesterol levels and higher HDL ("good") cholesterol levels

GETTING STARTED

Set Yourself Some S.M.A.R.T. Goals

S = Specific   **M** = Measurable   **A** = Attainable   **R** = Realistic   **T** = within a Time frame

- Stop making excuses. Everyone is busy, some more than others. The fact is, only you can exercise your body.
- Write a list of activities you enjoy doing or would like to try. What activities have you been successful with in the past?
- Use a calendar to book an appointment with yourself 3x week. Many people make the mistake of giving all their time to family and others, neglecting themselves.
- Have a problem staying committed? Work out with a friend who has similar goals, sign up for an exercise class or book a sitter on a regular basis.
- Write out a one week, a one month and a 3 month goal and post them where you can see them daily.

- Keep photos at your desk or on your computer desktop that motivate you to obtain your fitness goals.
- Workout with proper shoes, comfortable workout clothing, water bottle, etc.
- Have a positive attitude. Even athletes envision their success before they compete.
- Reward your successes with something you like such as training gloves, a new book, a movie, or a manicure.

Strength Training – Weight bearing exercise will build stronger muscles, lungs, joints and bones. It's no longer a young persons activity. Research shows that those over 65 years of age who exercise have a decreased risk of hip fractures.

- Include exercises for every major muscle group, including the muscles of the arms, chest, back, stomach, hips and legs.
- Beginners should start with 2-3 times a week while the more experienced may train 3-5 times a week.
- You need not join a fitness facility, many people chose to workout from home with a minimal amount of equipment.
- Consider hiring a certified trainer to put you on a program appropriate for your fitness level. Learning proper form can prevent possible injuries and set-backs.

Aerobic Exercise – Aerobic exercise does wonders for the cardiovascular system, improves the immune system, cholesterol levels, and blood pressure measurements, and decreases stress levels.

- All adults should exercise at least 30 minutes of moderate-intensity activity on most, if not all days of the week. You may also accumulate the time which means that you can do 10-15

minutes at a time and repeat that a couple of times throughout the day; for example, 10 minutes in the morning, 10 minutes at lunch, and 10 minutes around dinner.
- A moderate intensity is equivalent to feeling "warm and slightly out of breath" when you do it.
- Consider trying some of the following aerobic activities: walking, jogging, dancing, circuit weights, aerobics, dancing, swimming, using aerobic equipment, rope skipping, biking, skiing, snow-shoeing, skate-skiing, kick-boxing, etc.
- Purchase a pedometer or a heart rate monitor for added support.

Flexibility Exercise – Flexibility is needed to maintain joint range of motion and reduce the risk of injury and muscle soreness. Always warm up before you stretch. Stretching is not an activity meant to cause pain.

- Avoid bouncing and make sure you hold your stretch position for at least 15 to 20 seconds before moving back to your original position.
- Try stretching between weight training sets…this will utilize the recovery time you are taking and will make your workout more efficient.

SIMPLE STRATEGIES FOR "EXTRA STEPS"

- Park farther away from your destination.
- Take the stairs, not the elevator or escalator.
- Get off the bus a few blocks early.
- Exercise during commercial breaks.
- Walk during your breaks and lunch hour.
- Find a walking partner for the evening.
- Walk the golf course…don't ride!
- Walk the arena or field while your child is playing their sport.
- Play games with your children that include walking and running.
- Walk your dog, or even your neighbour's dog!

Always check with your doctor before beginning any exercise program, especially if you are over 40 or have cardiovascular risk factors, such as smoking, high blood pressure, high cholesterol, diabetes or a family history of heart disease.

IT IS NEVER TO LATE TO GET STARTED

Only you can make the decision to change your life and health for the better. That decision could

enable you to live a long, healthy life that is filled with active living well beyond retirement. We must face the fact that we are literally growing old before our time. When you nurture and support your body with regular exercise and healthy nutrition, your body reciprocates with more energy plus weight control. Taking care of your body, no matter what your age, is an investment. The return is priceless

KEEP HYDRATED: DRINK 6 TO 8 GLASSES OF WATER DAILY

We could only go a few days without water before our body would begin to deteriorate and die. Our bodies use water every day for all its internal cellular functions. It has been recommended that we have eight glasses of water every day to replenish what we have lost. Unfortunately, most people fall short on that prescription and may suffer from common complaints such as lack of energy, headaches, and sometimes even joint and muscle aches. When we exercise we need even more water to replace what is lost during a workout. This is the major cause of fatigue and poor performance. You might lose around 1 litre (or 33 ounces) of water in an hour workout so you will need to replace it before, during and after exercising or playing sports.

Shopping List

FRESH FOODS

MEAT/POULTRY
- ☐ Chicken breast
- ☐ Turkey breast
- ☐ Ground chicken
- ☐ Ground turkey
- ☐ Lean ground beef
- ☐ Lean cuts of beef
- ☐ Wild game
- ☐ Buffalo
- ☐ Pork loin
- ☐ Turkey bacon
- ☐ Canadian (back) bacon

FISH and SEAFOOD
- ☐ Salmon
- ☐ Tuna
- ☐ Trout
- ☐ Halibut
- ☐ Sole
- ☐ Shrimp

DAIRY, EGGS and SOY
- ☐ Skim or 1% milk
- ☐ Soy milk
- ☐ Tofu
- ☐ Eggs
- ☐ Low-fat sour cream
- ☐ Low-fat plain yogurt
- ☐ Low-fat cottage cheese
- ☐ Low-fat cheeses
- ☐ Feta cheese
- ☐ Parmesan cheese
- ☐ Ricotta cheese

VEGETABLES
- ☐ Leafy vegetables
- ☐ Artichokes
- ☐ Asparagus
- ☐ Broccoli
- ☐ Brussels sprouts
- ☐ Cabbage
- ☐ Carrots
- ☐ Cauliflower
- ☐ Celery
- ☐ Cucumber
- ☐ Peas
- ☐ Green pepper
- ☐ Red and orange
  bell peppers
- ☐ Snow peas
- ☐ Spinach
- ☐ Tomato
- ☐ Zucchini
- ☐ Yams
- ☐ Green onion
- ☐ Onions
- ☐ Small new potatoes
- ☐ Mushrooms
- ☐ Winter squash
- ☐ Frozen vegetables

FRESH HERBS
- ☐ Cilantro
- ☐ Parsley
- ☐ Mint
- ☐ Ginger
- ☐ Garlic

FRUITS
- ☐ Apples
- ☐ Blueberries
- ☐ Blackberries
- ☐ Strawberries
- ☐ Huckleberries
- ☐ Oranges
- ☐ Grapefruit
- ☐ Cherries
- ☐ Apricots
- ☐ Pears
- ☐ Peaches
- ☐ Grapes
- ☐ Pineapple
- ☐ Plums
- ☐ Kiwi fruit
- ☐ Bananas
- ☐ Lemons
- ☐ Limes
- ☐ Cranberries
- ☐ Mandarin oranges
- ☐ Mango
- ☐ Papaya
- ☐ Watermelon
- ☐ Cantaloupe
- ☐ Honeydew
- ☐ Raspberries

Extras _____

_____

_____

_____

_____

_____

_____

_____

PANTRY

GRAINS
- [ ] Black beans
- [ ] Chickpeas
- [ ] Kidney beans
- [ ] Pinto beans
- [ ] Soy beans
- [ ] Lentils
- [ ] Split peas
- [ ] Slow-cook oatmeal
- [ ] Cornmeal
- [ ] Whole wheat flour
- [ ] Bran
- [ ] Barley
- [ ] Buckwheat
- [ ] Bulgur
- [ ] Quinoa
- [ ] Basmati rice
- [ ] Brown rice
- [ ] Long grain rice, parboiled
- [ ] Wild rice
- [ ] Whole wheat kernels
- [ ] Whole rye kernels
- [ ] Sprouted wheat high fibre bread
- [ ] Whole wheat wraps
- [ ] Whole wheat and vegetable pasta

CEREAL
- [ ] High fibre cereal
- [ ] All Bran™
- [ ] Bran Buds™

STAPLES
- [ ] Soy or whey protein powder
- [ ] Low-glycemic meal replacement powder

CANNED GOODS
- [ ] Tuna/salmon
- [ ] Beets
- [ ] Corn
- [ ] Green/yellow beans
- [ ] Tomatoes
- [ ] Tomato paste
- [ ] Mushrooms
- [ ] Mandarin oranges
- [ ] Pineapple chunks
- [ ] Pumpkin

SPICES
- [ ] Salt
- [ ] Pepper
- [ ] Allspice
- [ ] Basil
- [ ] Celery Seed
- [ ] Chili powder
- [ ] Cinnamon
- [ ] Cloves
- [ ] Cumin
- [ ] Garlic powder
- [ ] Ground ginger
- [ ] Greek seasoning
- [ ] Italian spice
- [ ] Nutmeg
- [ ] Oregano
- [ ] Thyme
- [ ] Turmeric
- [ ] Dry mustard
- [ ] Hot pepper flakes
- [ ] Curry powder
- [ ] Curry paste
- [ ] Wasabi powder
- [ ] Chicken bouillon cubes
- [ ] Beef bouillon cubes

CONDIMENTS
- [ ] Low-fat mayonnaise
- [ ] Dijon mustard
- [ ] Lemon juice
- [ ] Balsamic vinegar
- [ ] Wine vinegar
- [ ] Hot sauce
- [ ] Worcestershire sauce
- [ ] Soy sauce
- [ ] Hoisin sauce
- [ ] Teriyaki sauce

NUTS and FATS
- [ ] Natural peanut butter
- [ ] Almonds
- [ ] Pecans
- [ ] Sesame seeds
- [ ] Walnuts
- [ ] Flaxseed (ground)
- [ ] Flaxseed oil
- [ ] Olive oil
- [ ] Canola oil
- [ ] Cooking spray

EXTRAS
- [ ] Raisins
- [ ] Dried cranberries
- [ ] Vanilla extract
- [ ] Almond extract
- [ ] Unflavoured gelatin
- [ ] Stevia
- [ ] Olives

Index

Acknowledgements

To our families and friends who gave of their time, energy and patience to make this project a reality, we offer our heartfelt appreciation. The success of *Low-Glycemic Meals in Minutes* is a result of team effort!

To Laura's family: Rob, Jake, Anya and Grandma Irene, and Cheryl's family: Noel, Aaron, Evan and her mother Colene, we thank you for all your support and patience while we worked the many hours needed to get the project done. A special thanks to Aaron who came home at lunch to test our creations and help us with our computer glitches.

Deepest appreciation to Kelly Pape, our food photographer who spent long hours shooting pictures, editing and food styling, but most of all for all the laughs we had in the process. Her photographic expertise has brought our recipes to life.

Hats off to Sheryl Giudici, R.D., who was instrumental with recipe testing, editing and nutrition review. We appreciate the practical application of the cookbook with her clients at the nutrition clinic. To this end, we have dedicated page 16 to some tips that have helped inspire her clients to make healthy lifestyle choices. We also want to thank her daugher Christina Giudici, R.D., for her assistance in designing the sample menu plan.

Special thanks to Gaye Dunkley for compiling the index, to Goldie Preziosi for proof reading the final drafts, and to Teresa Meierhofer for her food styling flair. To all the families and friends who contributed success stories, we thank you for your inspirational messages.

A special thank you to our Team Vitality for their ongoing support and encouragement, and particularly for the recipe testing and fun times we shared at potlucks and socials enjoying our low-glycemic recipes. And yes, tofu lasagna does taste good.

A bouquet of roses to the team at Wayside Press, especially Glenda Mathew, our graphic designer whose editorial and design expertise moved us along quickly, particularly with revisions for the third printing of the cookbook.

And to our mentor, Ray D. Strand, M.D., for his guidance, inspiration and support to provide a practical tool that will assist people with the skills to make low-glycemic meal preparation easy: the healthy choice also needs to be the easy choice — and we thank Dr. Strand for paving the way with his educational books and resources.